FREEDOM
from BUSYNESS

Biblical Help for Overloaded People

Michael Zigarelli

LifeWay Press®

Nashville, Tennessee

ISBN 1-4158-2581-5

This book is a resource in the Personal Life category
of the Christian Growth Study Plan.
Course CG-1169

Dewey Decimal Classification: 640
Subject Headings: TIME MANAGEMENT \ CHRISTIAN LIFE \ STRESS (PSYCHOLOGY)

Unless otherwise noted, all Scripture quotations are taken from the Holman Christian Standard
Bible®, copyright © 1999, 2000, 2002, 2003 by Holman Bible Publishers.
Used by permission. Holman Christian Standard Bible®, Holman CSB®, and HCSB®
are federally registered trademarks of Holman Bible Publishers.
Scripture quotations identified NIV are from the Holy Bible, New International Version,
copyright © 1973, 1978, 1984 by International Bible Society. Used by permission.

To order additional copies of this resource: WRITE LifeWay Church Resources Customer Service;
One LifeWay Plaza; Nashville, TN 37234-0113;
FAX order to (615) 251-5933; PHONE (800) 458-2772; ORDER ONLINE at
www.lifeway.com; or VISIT the LifeWay Christian Store serving you.

Printed in the United States of America

Leadership and Adult Publishing
LifeWay Church Resources
One LifeWay Plaza
Nashville, TN 37234-0175

Dedication

For my kids,
Michael, Laura, Sarah and Zachary,
who, without saying a word,
taught me the importance
of not being too busy.

Acknowledgements

Proverbs says that "Plans fail for lack of counsel, but with many advisors they succeed" (15:22, NIV). Indeed, I've been blessed with more than my fair share of advisors for this project. Foremost, I'm indebted to God for delivering the ideas and words I needed exactly when I needed them, usually around 4:30 in the morning. Also, thanks to my wife Tara for her careful review of the work (somewhat later than 4:30 a.m.) and for helping shape this so it speaks to women as much as it speaks to men.

I can't say enough about the talent, the work ethic and the dedication of my new friends at LifeWay. Throughout this project, I've appreciated Jim Johnston's brainstorming, Bill Craig's confidence that a business professor could write a busyness resource, Tim Davis's and Cindy McClain's market insights, Connie Eubanks's meticulous copy editing, and especially Sam House's editorial smoothing and project management skills. I'm also grateful to the LifeWay film and production crew—Betsy Wedekind, Bill Cox, Tim Cox, Steve Fralick, and Paul Lopez—and to the audio book director, Mike Psanos, for helping this novice sound like a professional and feel like a member of the family. All of you LifeWay folks exude excellence and it's been a tremendous blessing to co-labor with you on *Freedom from Busyness*. You, my "many advisors," have truly made this project a success!

About the Author

Michael Zigarelli lives in Virginia with his wife Tara and their four children. This Christian husband and father holds a Ph.D. from Rutgers University. He is the Dean of the Regent University School of Business, author of several books and many articles. He is the founding editor of *Regent Business Review,* an online magazine for Christian leaders and managers, and the creator of Christianity9to5.org and Assess-Yourself.org.

An expert in management and ethics, Mike's writings have been translated internationally. He has appeared on dozens of Christian radio broadcasts and has been interviewed by *The New York Times, Time Magazine* and *The Washington Post.*

Contents

Preface

I remember reading a quote from C.S. Lewis about his experience in writing *The Screwtape Letters,* his insightful little volume about Satan's tactics. Lewis said that in order to understand and convey accurately how Satan operates, he essentially had to descend into that world—to project himself into a world devoid of all beauty and civility. That process, Lewis reported, almost overwhelmed him.

Yet, that process yielded such a profound and enduring work. As a writer, I found that quote intriguing when I first read it. Now, though, on the back end of this project on busyness, Lewis' words have taken on fresh meaning for me.

Like Lewis, I've lived in the sometimes-dark world about which I write, both before and during this project. My cup of responsibility runneth over and over the past decade. I'm a husband. I'm a father of four grade school kids. I'm a professor and a business school dean. I'm a magazine editor and a freelance writer. I own a small business. Looking back, I've taken on too much. Some seasons, way too much.

Then, in the midst of that frenetic life, along comes this opportunity to create a study for LifeWay, an organization I've always admired greatly.

As hard as overload has been for me in recent years, I think it's shaped this study in positive ways. The suggestions I offer are informed not only by exegesis and empirical research, but also by painful first-hand experience of an over-extended life. The upshot, I hope, is a set of reflections and recommendations that drill beneath the superficial to some of the real issues.

My premise—and the assumption that underlies my passion on this issue—is this: for too many Christians, the busyness and pace of our lives are primary obstacles to living the life God wants us to live. When we look back in our old age, many of us will regret how our busy lives crowded out God, crowded out the people we love, crowded out joyful service, and crowded out the quality of life God wanted to give to us.

The real tragedy of it all, though, would be reflecting in our rocking chairs about how preventable the overload was. We had the keys to our shackles the whole time, but we never used them because we didn't even realize we were in shackles.

There's an alternative future, one that will leave us with no such regrets. It's a future of a life well-lived, of a life free from the bondage of busyness, of a life that maintains balance, boundaries and God-honoring priorities.

That's the vision of this study and its accompanying video curriculum—to help you examine whether you're bound by busyness and handcuffed by hurry, to offer some insights into how to live a better life, and to remove a major obstacle to the joyful and peace-filled life God promises.

Sound refreshing? As one who's turned a corner on this lifestyle, let me assure you, it is. But like so many things in the Christian life, this journey begins with a paradox: to gain time, you have to lose some. To make real, lasting progress, you'll need to invest time over the next thirty days—time to examine the problem; time to experiment with some Bible-based solutions; time to work with an accountability partner; most importantly, time to hear from God on this issue.

It'll be your wisest investment of the year, though. Invest the next thirty days and forever trade your busy life for a better life.

Michael Zigarelli
Virginia Beach, Virginia
January 2006

THE BONDAGE
OF BUSYNESS

An Epidemic Among Christians

But seek first the kingdom of God and His righteousness, and all these things will be provided for you. Matthew 6:33

Two thousand years after the Great Physician healed us through the cross, there appears to be an epidemic affecting His followers. Some call it "busyness"— busyness to the point of overload, busyness to the point of habitual hurry, even busyness that's led to ignoring the Physician Himself.

Consider some of the evidence of this epidemic from a recent survey I did of about 13,000 believers worldwide.[1]
- To the statement: "The busyness of my life gets in the way of developing my relationship with God," six out of ten (60%) responded that this is often or always true of them.
- To the statement "I rush from task to task," more than four out of ten (43%) said this is often or always true of them.
- About half (49%) said they often or always eat quickly, and about one in three (30%) admitted that they often or always "hurry even when I don't have to hurry."

Those are staggering numbers. It appears that many of us Christians are doing way too many things at a pace that's way too fast. As a result, we're distracted from God and we're overloaded, even exhausted. In fact, one out of two Christians (51%) in my survey said that they're often or always "exhausted at the end of my day," and another 24% said this is true of them sometimes. That's a lot of tired Christians.

Let me suggest something that I don't think is very controversial: this is not the life God wants us to live. He wants His children to live healthy lives, just as we want for our own children. Not lives that are too busy for a relationship with Him. Not lives of running from one responsibility to the next. Not lives that later regret what we missed while we were diligently completing our to-do lists. The Doctor's orders are for us to trade the busy life for a better life.

Does that sound at all inviting to you? If so, this study may help.

It's not a study about managing your time better so you can get everything done. Neither is it intended to help you organize your activities so you can get more done in less time. There are plenty of very good "busyness management" resources on the market, if that's your goal. Instead, this study is about busyness reduction—permanent escape from too much activity, too many responsibilities, too much hurry, and too little God.

To get there, this study will walk you through a process of considering how you invest your time and how God might want you to invest it differently, to yield a higher quality of life. To yield a life that puts Him first. To yield a life where important relationships are no longer compromised. To yield a life of peace and joy. Finally.

This study will also help you create a plan of action and encourage an accountability relationship, so that the lessons God teaches you in the next thirty days are more likely to stick. Many Christians have taken a few steps up this escape route, only to slide back to the start because of old habits or lack of support. Having a plan and an encourager will enable you to maintain traction, long after this study ends.

Indeed, there's an epidemic of busyness that's infected the body of Christ. It's separating us from God and from one another. And it's separating us from the consistently joyful life God wants to give us. If you see yourself in the statistics above, take heart. The Great Physician sees you as a candidate for His permanent cure!

Think About It

To what extent is the busyness of your life compromising your relationship with God?

To what extent is it compromising other important relationships in your life?

For Group Discussion

What do you think God would like you to get out of this study? Write down one or two things here and indicate whether you're really committed to partnering with God throughout this study to reach these goals.

Talk to God About It

Consider the familiar Scripture: "Seek first the kingdom of God and His righteousness, and all these things will be provided for you" (Matt. 6:33). Reflect on the busyness of your life. Take a few minutes to ask God whether the busyness of your life might be a result of reversing this teaching; that is, seeking the good things of life before seeking God.

Your Freedom from Busyness Plan, Part 1

If you did not complete the diagnostic survey that accompanies this study, today would be a good day to do that. It will help you answer the question, "How much of an obstacle is busyness to my growth as a Christian and to the life God wants me to lead?" Begin your Freedom from Busyness plan with a benchmark; that is, begin this plan by writing down your busyness score from this assessment and what you think that score means.

---

[1]Michael A. Zigarelli, *The Obstacles to Growth Survey*, 2002. All rights reserved.

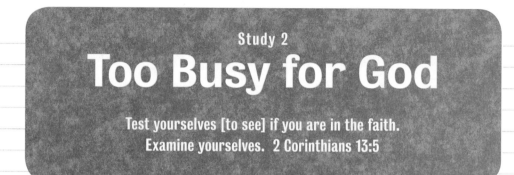

Too Busy for God

Test yourselves [to see] if you are in the faith.
Examine yourselves. 2 Corinthians 13:5

On my way to work, I drive by a church that's known for, among other things, selling fruit. I'm not sure why the church does this. Maybe it's to create another revenue stream or perhaps there's something symbolic in the idea. But regardless, they sell fruit.

Driving by one day, I saw a striking sign near the roadside in front of the church. In large letters, the sign read: "No fruit this month."

I knew what the sign meant, of course, since I was familiar with the church. They wouldn't be vending citrus for a few weeks. But the irony of those words outside a church—"no fruit this month"—had apparently escaped the pastor.

How true these words are for some churches and for some of us believers. We go through the motions of our faith but produce "no fruit," no significant evidence that we belong to God. It's not that we don't want to bear fruit. Most of us do. Rather, our barrenness is a natural result of busyness. We're so focused on our endless to-do lists that we ignore God. And no God this month means no fruit this month.

The better outcome is something you may have heard a thousand times: "The fruit of the Spirit is love, joy, peace, patience, kindness, goodness, faith, gentleness, self-control" (Gal. 5:22-23). Are these qualities that describe you? More to the point, do they characterize you recently? Or might it be accurate to have a sign on your back that says "no fruit this month"?

Being a Christian means having the courage to ask yourself the tough questions and to answer those questions with naked honesty. Proverbs 14:8 says "the sensible man's wisdom is to consider his way." Similarly, Paul instructs the Corinthians to "test yourselves [to see] if you are in the faith" (2 Cor. 13:5) and the Galatians that "each person should examine his own work" (Gal. 6:4). Indeed, self-examination is a spiritual discipline.

Being Christian also means responding to what God reveals through our self-examination by making better choices in the future. It means to change. If we're over-extended, though, we have a tendency to ignore this reality-to ignore that we've become so busy that we're distracted from God. Busyness is the chain saw that severs our branch from His vine. Is it any wonder we see so little fruit?

If you haven't experienced much improvement lately in the fruit of the Spirit, maybe it's time to ask whether you've become too busy for God.

Think About It

Are you too busy for God? In other words, is the busyness of your life distracting you from developing your relationship with God?

If this is a problem for you, no recommendation in this study will be effective unless you address this problem.

For Group Discussion

Here's another way to assess whether there's a problem: How much has your prayer life improved in the past six months?

How about in the past year?

If it's not improving, explain whether or not it's because you've been too busy or distracted to talk with God.

Talk to God About It

Consider Paul's admonition to "pray constantly" (1 Thess. 5:17). Surely Paul can't mean that we have to spend every waking moment on our knees. Reflect on what else this could mean, how you could honor this call to action, and how an overloaded life gets in the way of doing God's will here.

Your Freedom from Busyness Plan, Part 2

When you're having a particularly busy or overloaded day, which attribute of the fruit of the Spirit seems to suffer the most?

How do you see that affecting the people around you, and what will you do to change that?

Too Busy for Your Marriage

This is why a man leaves his father and mother and bonds with his wife, and they become one flesh. Genesis 2:24

"If I died today, I don't think my wife would miss me one bit."

Scott was opening up to me about his lackluster twelve-year marriage, and I knew that on this issue, he was being prophetic. His priorities were not God's priorities, and consequently, his relationship with Sherri was dying.

"Really?" I responded to Scott, trying to seem at least a little surprised.

"Oh, she'd miss my paycheck," he continued, blending sadness with frustration. "And I'm sure she'd miss things I do for her and the kids. But she wouldn't miss *me*. I bet it would take her less than a week to recover after my funeral."

Knowing what I did about Scott's workaholic tendencies, I took a relational risk.

"Well, you might be right about that," I said to his dismay. I think he was expecting me to disagree with him. "But a year from now everything can be completely different—if you want it to be. Invest more time in your marriage. It'll become a lot healthier, and Sherri would probably love you a lot more."

I forged ahead and made my recommendation more specific. "Let me suggest something. Commit to spend an hour or two a day with her, just the two of you.

If you're serious about turning a corner on this thing, you need some daily quality time together. Non-negotiable time. Fun time. Alone time. Every day."

I could see that Scott was incredulous at the recommendation. "I'd love to spend more time with Sherri. But an hour or two *each day?* Between the sixty-hour-a-week job and time with the kids, Sherri and I are lucky if we get fifteen minutes."

"Then quit your job," I said flatly. It was a logical conclusion. "Or keep the job and work a lot fewer hours so that you can give more of yourself to Sherri."

Scott looked at me like I was from Pluto. I looked back at him and told him he had been making a choice, and an unwise one at that. He said nothing. I gave him an encouraging smile. "You know I'm right, my friend. It's entirely your choice."

For most of us, our marriages are what we make of them. When we choose to busy ourselves with other things, we're choosing not to invest in our spouse. This is a far cry from the biblical ideal of husbands loving their wives as "Christ loved the church" and of wives submitting to their husbands as to the Lord (Eph. 5:22-33).

The flip side of the story is that Sherri also had been making choices. This stay-at-home mom invested countless hours each week caring for her kids, supervising homework, running them around to activities, buying them stuff, and generally trying to give them the best possible childhood. She also poured herself into various community service and church-related activities. And through it all, she spent almost no time thinking about improving her marriage or making Scott happier.

Indeed, reaping and sowing was in full operation here, but truth be told, Sherri was choosing her work over her marriage in the same way that Scott was. Since many of Sherri's friends chose similar priorities, it was a way of life Sherri thought was completely normal. Lonely and exhausting perhaps, but normal.

Now, as a father of four, I do understand that Sherri can't just quit her kids like someone can quit a job. But I can tell you that if she put the same creativity and energy into her marriage as she does into her kids and service activities, she'd be astonished with the result. Same with Scott. He's a creative and energetic guy—when focused on his job, when coaching soccer, or when serving on a church committee. Everywhere, it seems, except with his marriage. Bad choice. Terrible choice, in fact.

Priorities are what we do. They are where we invest our time. One remedy for Scott and Sherri's mediocre marriage is for them to choose to make it better, whatever it takes. The choice is to change their priorities so that they reflect God's priorities.

What about you? How do you choose to spend your time? How much effort are you really expending to make your marriage great? How much creativity and energy do you invest to delight your spouse everyday? How often do you think and pray about what it would take to become "one flesh" in your marriage (Gen. 2:24)? If your priorities are not what God wants them to be, why not vow to change that now?

Think About It
How often in a month do you pray for your marriage? This is a strong indicator of its importance to you. Compare this to how often you pray for other things.

For Group Discussion
If "Priorities are what we do," in a typical day, how much of a "priority" is it for you to delight in your spouse and to make your marriage as good as God wants it to be?

Talk to God About It
Consider, "This is why a man leaves his father and mother and bonds with his wife, and they become one flesh" (Gen. 2:24). Reflect on what God means by "one flesh." What does God want you to do in pursuit of this calling?

Your Freedom from Busyness Plan, Part 3
What does your spouse really want? What choices will you make in your life to serve your spouse as God wants you to? Go ahead and write in the margins.

Too Busy for Other People

He gives strength to the weary and strengthens the powerless. Youths may faint and grow weary, and young men stumble and fall, but those who trust in the LORD will renew their strength; they will soar on wings like eagles; they will run and not grow weary; they will walk and not faint. Isaiah 40:29-31

Have you noticed how bad service is these days? From department store workers to customer service reps to cable repairmen, service stinks. And then there's the department of motor vehicles (DMV). I'm convinced that these folks hold meetings to devise diabolical new ways to increase our wait time.

Of course, there are plenty of exceptions. Some service people are exemplary. But, I think many of us have come to expect poor service from almost everyone.

But do *we* provide poor service as well? We have opportunities to serve each day— co-workers or customers, an elderly parent, a spouse and children, other drivers in traffic. How's your service? Great? Or is it closer to what we get at the DMV?

If you're like a lot of folks, it's probably somewhere in between. Though we're called to be like Jesus and wash people's feet with humility and gladness, we fall short of that ideal daily. Sometimes far short. And sometimes hourly.

It's not just our hard-wiring. Let me introduce you to another reason, related to our busyness, that some of us struggle with servanthood. Psychologists have documented a condition that affects people who do a lot of serving. It may sound like psycho-babble to you—like the disorder dú jour we hear about on the nightly news—but this one's backed up by some decent research. It's called "compassion fatigue." It means, in simple terms, that you've been so busy taking care of others that you're now experiencing a decline in your ability to feel compassion for them. It's a form of burnout. People in the "helping professions" and service industries are especially at risk—people like counselors, caregivers, teachers, social workers, pastors, parents —just about anyone whose primary job is to respond to others' needs. The more we push ourselves beyond healthy limits to minister to others, the more susceptible we are to losing compassion for them.

After several intense hours, days, and weeks of taking care of other people's problems, we can grow weary of it. Even if we like or love these people, overload starts to set in and serving them loses its joy. When the intensity persists over longer periods of time—months or years—we may even feel like we want to withdraw from people altogether (psychologists call this "depersonalization," if you want the fancy term). Service to others has now become a burden rather than a blessing.

Notice the connection to busyness. We're so busy serving that eventually we become exhausted—mentally, physically, and even spiritually. We don't have an attitude problem or some deep-seated spiritual deficiency. We may just have this thing called compassion fatigue. It explains a lot about the service we receive today, as well as the service we provide to others.

Understanding the problem is an empowering first step toward doing something about it, so let me suggest just that. Understand it. Watch yourself for signs of this condition. If you're heroically caring for others' needs so often that you're becoming jaded toward their needs, you probably should scale back your service (Week 2 of this study goes into detail about how to do this in a Christian manner.)

Let me also recommend that you invite God into those relationships and into those moments of "depersonalization"—of compassion fatigue to the point of wanting to withdraw from others. The Bible indicates that He will sustain you. Isaiah, in particular, says that God "gives strength to the weary and strengthens the powerless. Youths may faint and grow weary, and young men stumble and fall, but those who trust in the Lord will renew their strength" (Isa. 40: 29-31).

Over the next twenty-four hours, look for signs of compassion fatigue in yourself. If you find any, ask God to strengthen you and to give you fresh perspective about how blessed you are to have your ministry to others.

Watch for the problem in others, as well. Chances are you'll see it often in just the next day. Consider asking God's blessing on these people as well, rather than reacting as you normally do when experiencing bad service. You may be surprised by the power He'll give you to be a light to the beleaguered cashier, the unfriendly nurse, and even the window agent you waited 90 minutes to see at the DMV!

Think About It
How does it make you feel when you've served someone with excellence?

For Group Discussion
How does your busyness affect your ability to serve others joyfully and well?

Talk to God About It
Reflect on Isaiah 40:29-31, cited in today's lesson, to seek practical ways you can co-labor with God to gain more time, energy, and willingness to serve people.

Your Freedom from Busyness Plan, Part 4
In the next 24 hours, watch for compassion fatigue symptoms—like a lack of empathy for people's problems or a desire to withdraw from them. Before doing the next study in this book, write your observations. How big of a problem is compassion fatigue for you? What are two things you can do to begin addressing the problem?

Lend a Hand During This Study

Therefore encourage one another and build each other up
as you are already doing. 1 Thessalonians 5:11

He was freezing to death. And all he could see was black.

On top of that, Lawrence was suffocating. "I tried to push at the snow to enable
me to breathe but only managed a few millimeters," he later told the media.
"I desperately tried to get some air."

The Alps in January can be a perilous place. Now, buried alive by an avalanche,
Lawrence was about to die. Several feet above him, his fellow snowboarders franti-
cally tried to locate a signal from his avalanche beacon, technology designed for
just this situation. They knew they had precious few moments to rescue their friend.

After three full minutes, it looked hopeless. But then—suddenly, miraculously—there
it was. The signal! The group dug feverishly and soon they reached Lawrence's hand,
frozen solid. Pulling him out, Danny, a surgeon, found a weak pulse and began to
resuscitate Lawrence, ultimately saving his life as he had done for so many others
back at the hospital.[2]

When Lawrence was in need, his friends responded heroically. That's what friends
do. They come to the rescue, even when our cries for help aren't audible.

A lot of people around you are silently buried, too. Not with snow, of course. With work. With responsibility. With activity. With debt. With a suffocating lifestyle that has consumed them like an avalanche and left them gasping for air.

Like Lawrence, they need someone's help to escape their predicament. Like Danny, you may be in just the right position to help.

Escaping the busyness and overload of our lives—and remaining free from it—is a challenging task. In fact, for many people, it may be an impossible task to accomplish alone. That's where you come in. "Encourage one another and build each other up" Paul says in his encouraging letter to the Thessalonians (1 Thess. 5:11). It's a message we hear throughout Scripture, but hear too seldom today.

It won't take a sophisticated avalanche beacon to locate such people. They're all around you, and more than likely, you know who they are. But if you don't know, simply ask. If you're doing this study as part of a group, ask who among the group wants an encourager and an accountability partner.

It's possible that no one will speak up—people who are buried alive tend to be silent—but the expression on someone's face is his or her beacon. Connect with this person and lend a hand to pull him or her out.

And in the same way, if overload has become a problem for you, allow someone to give you a hand up, too. Pair up with someone beginning this week—someone who will support you in this study, someone who will pray with you and for you, someone who will care enough to ask you whether you're really making the daily studies a priority and whether you're making progress to reduce the busyness of your life. There's no shame in getting assistance when you're snowed under. In fact, sometimes it's the only way out.

Just ask Lawrence.

Think About It

How often would you like to talk with an accountability/encouragement partner in this study about busyness and overload, and your progress in dealing with both?

For Group Discussion

A lot of Christians throughout the centuries have indicated that we're more likely to experience permanent change when we have an accountability partner who can support us and ask us the tough questions. What do you think?

Talk to God About It

When Jesus sent out the disciples to spread the good news of the kingdom, He sent them out two by two (Luke 10:1). When He taught about prayer, He said "where two or three are gathered together in My name, I am there among them" (Matt. 18:20). What , if anything, does this tell us about the impact of partnering with someone to effect change?

Your Freedom from Busyness Plan, Part 5

Write down the names of some people with whom you might partner for accountability and encouragement during this study. It would also be a good idea to seek God's help in identifying the right person or people.

---

[2]Geoff Green, "Businessman rescued after preparing to die: Snowboarder buried alive in avalanche nightmare," *Manchester Evening News* (U.K.), January 31, 2001.

FREEDOM THROUGH SAYING NO

The Bible on Saying No

But Ruth replied: Do not persuade me to leave you or go back and not follow you. For wherever you go, I will go, and wherever you live, I will live; your people will be my people, and your God will be my God. Ruth 1:16

If you ever thought it unbiblical to say no to people you care about, here's a list you might want to hang on your refrigerator:

- To say yes to God's directive to deliver Israel from bondage, Moses had to say no to caring for his family (Ex. 3-4).

- To say yes to remaining in Bethlehem with Naomi, her mother-in-law, Ruth had to say no to living out the rest of her life with her friends and relatives in Moab (Ruth 1).

- To say yes to keeping her promise to God, Hannah had to say no to raising her son, Samuel (1 Sam. 1).

- To say yes to protecting his friend David, Jonathan had to say no to the wishes of his father, King Saul (1 Sam. 20).

- To say yes to rebuilding Jerusalem's wall, Nehemiah had to say no to serving King Artaxerxes (Neh. 1-2).

- To say yes to God's call to marry a prostitute—and to then remarry her after she strayed—Hosea said no to marrying women he might have preferred more (Hos. 1-3).

- To say yes to God's command to name her baby John, Elizabeth had to say no to friends and relatives who insisted that she abide by tradition and name the baby after someone in the family (Luke 1:57-61).

- To say yes to following Jesus, the disciples had to say no to remaining with their families.

- To say yes to listening to Jesus, Mary had to say no to helping her sister Martha (Luke 10).

- To say yes to God's command to convert the Gentiles, Saul (later Paul) had to say no to the wishes of everyone from his former life (Acts 9).

- To say yes to giving young John Mark a second chance, Barnabas had to say no to good relations and to continued travel with Paul (Acts 15:36-41).

- To say yes to ministering to those on the other side of the lake, Jesus had to say no to people in Galilee who wanted him to stay (Matt. 8:18).

Moses, Ruth, Hannah, Jonathan, Nehemiah, Hosea, Elizabeth, the disciples, Mary, Paul, Barnabas, Jesus. You could, no doubt, add others to the list as well. Throughout the Bible, we see people making hard choices to respond faithfully to God's will. We see people saying no to good things so that they can say yes to other good things.

So why do we think it's somehow un-Christian to do the same?

Think About It

Consider the question that closes this study: Why do we think it's somehow un-Christian to say no to people? What's your answer to that question?

For Group Discussion

What are your biggest obstacles to saying no to requests for your time, and what might you do to overcome those obstacles?

Talk to God About It

Scan through the above list of Bible figures who said no, and ask God to help you remember that sometimes saying no to a request is the most godly thing that we can do. In that prayer, ask God to give you discernment—to help you separate those opportunities He wants you to accept from those He does not want you to accept.

Your Freedom from Busyness Plan, Part 6

List some time-consuming things to which you've said yes, when, for the sake of boundaries, God may have wanted you to say no. If any of those obligations continue, what's your plan and your timetable for stepping away from them?

Give Yourself Permission to Say No

The Lord answered her, "Martha, Martha, you are worried and upset about many things, but one thing is necessary. Mary has made the right choice, and it will not be taken away from her." Luke 10:41–42

Martha went back to the kitchen choking back tears. *How could He be the Son of God and give an answer like that?* Jesus' words echoed endlessly through her head: "'*Martha, Martha, you are worried and upset about many things, ... Mary has chosen what is better'*" (Luke 10:41–42, NIV).

"Chosen what is better!" she grumbled, slamming a pot. "Sitting around is better than helping me prepare the meal? Does He think the food's going to appear miraculously like manna from heaven? Or maybe He's planning on whipping up something from nothing, like he did on the mountainside." She wiped her eyes and went back to her cutting board. Alone. Fuming. Disillusioned.

Of course, Luke doesn't tell us what happened after Jesus' instruction to Martha (Luke 10), but it's not hard to imagine Martha storming back to the kitchen because, frankly, that's what we might do. We're not very teachable when things seem unfair. So although Jesus gave her permission to stop fussing with dinner, I'd guess that Martha may not have given herself permission.

If God gave you permission to say no to some of the things that are overloading you, would you still do them anyway? Would you respond as our hypothetical Martha above? Or, would you choose "better" over "busier"?

When questions like these are just words on a page, the answers seem obvious. Of course we'd give ourselves permission, we respond dismissively. Who wouldn't do that? When it comes to actually making hard choices, though, we sometimes find out that *we* wouldn't do that.

Consider the requests for our time we encounter every week—requests for worthy efforts or requests voiced by people may know and care about—and consider how difficult it seems to say no to them. A relative asks you to baby-sit on Saturday night. Your daughter asks you to coach her softball team. A troop leader asks whether you can cover for him at the Boy Scout meeting. A pastor asks you to work in the church nursery, to teach Sunday school, or to serve on as a deacon. A teacher asks you to assist at school once a week. A friend asks you to counsel someone who might benefit from your experience. A coworker asks you to pitch in voluntarily with a project that's behind schedule.

These are all great service opportunities and the foot washer in us says it's time to grab a basin and towel and get to work. And it might be, for some of these requests. But perhaps God wants us to set some appropriate boundaries—to wash ten feet this season, not twenty or thirty.

The truth is that sometimes God does give us permission to say no to serving others. We saw that in Study 6. But when He does, we have a role to play, too: we have to give *ourselves* permission to say no. We have to put down the pot, shed the apron, and be still, confident that God will find another way to meet the need that we're not going to meet.

Until we escape the tyranny of the "automatic yes"—that is, until we give ourselves permission to say no to serving others—the overload will persist. In fact, it will likely get worse, since the more we say yes, the more people will ask of us.

If there's one area where Christians are under-taught, it's this one. Perhaps that's because it's so easy to hear these words as heresy. But teaching that it's okay to set boundaries around our service is not heretical, if our motivation for those boundaries is right—if our motivation is to have the space to do with excellence and joy what God wants us to do.

When your life is overloading you, give yourself permission to say no to new requests. It's not a sin and it's not un-Christian. Quite the opposite. It's choosing what's better.

Think About It
What are two time-consuming things you agreed to do, even though you didn't have the time to do them?

Why didn't you give yourself permission to say no to these requests?

For Group Discussion
Saying no to serving others is appropriate if God first gives us permission to say no to them. How will you know whether God is giving you permission to say no to a request for your time?

Talk to God About It
Read again the story of Martha and Mary in Luke 10. Take some time to explore with God what's stopping you from embracing Jesus' teaching to choose time with Him over more activity.

Your Freedom from Busyness Plan, Part 7
List a non-negotiable priority that you will not neglect when people request more of your time.

What's your plan for saying no when you encounter a worthy need that would compromise this non-negotiable?

Say No to Perfectionism

For am I now trying to win the favor of people, or God? Or am I striving to please people? If I were still trying to please people, I would not be a slave of Christ. Galatians 1:10

I like to hire perfectionists. They're people who usually get stuff right. They're people you can count on to deliver great work almost every time. They do much more than I would ever ask of them to ensure excellence. I love these people.

Unfortunately, though, they pay the price, and I have to remain vigilant to keep them from burning out. I tell them what I'm telling you right now: For all the wonderful things our perfectionism offers, it's often unnecessary. Sometimes it's even detrimental. In our work, we need to adopt a healthy theology of good enough, and move on to something else that matters more.

There are times when our work needs to be completely error-free, but not every task needs to be performed at that level. Recognize that "good enough" is a relative standard that depends on the task at hand. Sometimes 80 percent of our best is actually better stewardship than 100 percent.

That "80 percent principle" applies in other contexts as well. Consider the household. Our houses don't need to be perfectly clean—ever. Not even when we're expecting guests. If a guest raises an eyebrow, just tell him, "Sorry, we live here." Similarly, our lawns don't need to be weed-free or perfectly manicured. God put us on this earth to do more important things.

Our meals don't need to be perfectly cooked, either, or served at the perfect temperature. If we will adopt the standard of "good enough," if we'd just be genuinely grateful for the food and pray for those who live on one meal a day, it would open our eyes to how trivial our mealtime concerns are.

Our clothes, our hair, our bodies ... many people invest lots of time in these things to get them just right. But if our self-image is driven by what others think of us, we may feel worthy of love and respect only when we perform with perfection or when we look perfect. Stated differently, perfectionist tendencies may simply be the result of an unhealthy—even prideful—focus on reputation, good-standing with others, or people-pleasing, as the Apostle Paul puts it (Gal. 1:10). Perfectionism supports the belief that *our value as a person depends on what others think of us.*

The antidote is to believe, finally and forever, the familiar, bedrock Scriptures of God's unconditional love, regardless of your accomplishments and despite your flaws and failings. God loved you so much that He gave His only Son for you (John 3:16). There is no condemnation of you if you are in Christ Jesus (Rom. 8:1). " 'Come to me,' " Jesus says, all of you who are weary and burdened, and I will give you rest" (Matt. 11:28). These Scriptures indicate that your value has nothing to do with your accomplishments, your perfection, or what others think of you.

The second pill in God's antidote is to *respond* to His unconditional love by choosing God-pleasing over people-pleasing in everything you do—when you work, when you drive, when you shop, when you talk to people, when you experience some injustice, when you give, when you pray aloud, when you decide what you'll do with your day. Take seriously the calling to be exclusively a God-pleaser: "Am I now trying to win the favor of people, or God?" writes Paul. "If I were still trying to please people, I would not be a slave of Christ" (Gal. 1:10). Follow Paul's advice and everything will be different in your life tomorrow.

We live in a world that says, "Be concerned about what others think and then they'll love you." We worship a God who says, "Be concerned only about what I think—and I already love you." Seek perfection only in God's eyes. You'll be surprised at how that can lighten your load.

Think About It

If you have perfectionist tendencies, write down why you're working so hard to get everything just right. Is the real driver to get others to think well of you? It's easy to say no to this last question when the reality is yes, so you may want to talk this through with some people who know you well and whose opinions you trust.

For Group Discussion

Whether you'd label yourself a perfectionist or not, consider the central question in today's study: Is "people-pleasing" part of what's driving your overloaded schedule? Write down and share a time when this has happened.

Talk to God About It

Perfectionist tendencies are both an asset and a liability. Ask God to help you see when your perfectionism gets in the way of more important things and when it's encroaching on the quality of others' lives and your own.

Your Freedom from Busyness Plan, Part 8

What are three things in which you invest lots of time to get "just right" when perhaps from God's perspective, they don't need to be "just right"?

What's your plan for using the "80 percent principle" for these three items?

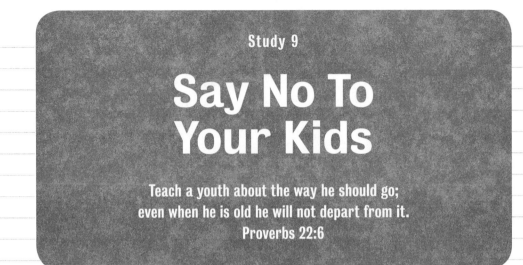

Say No To Your Kids

Teach a youth about the way he should go;
even when he is old he will not depart from it.
Proverbs 22:6

Out of the mouths of babes comes unbelievable stuff these days. Have you heard the way some kids talk to their parents? I listen in amazement at the mall, at carnivals, in the grocery store. Without a doubt, the spoiled-from-birth inmates are running their asylums—and running their parents ragged in the process. Many a mom and dad in the new millennium is more attendant than parent, shuttling kids daily from activity to activity, yielding regularly to their cries for fast food, over-buying for Christmas, cooking them separate meals because they won't eat what's put in front of them, photographing and videotaping every square inch of childhood. Some call it over-indulgence; others call it over-parenting. Regardless the label, it's overloading parents as never before.

The cause of parental overload goes beyond doing too much for our kids, though. Many contemporary parents also require too little of their kids. It now seems to be the exceptional child who helps out around the house without being told.

Case in point: Recently, a Mother's Day feature story in my local newspaper reported mothers' answers to the question, What do you really want for Mother's Day? Alongside pleas for "no breakfast in bed (the kitchen mess is not an attractive trade-off)" and for "a day with no screaming," there was this response: "I am always having to pick up after my entire family. So it would be really nice if for one day, they would pick up after themselves. I think my house would be spotless if they did—if they would just clean up their spaces for an entire day."

Can you imagine mothers from generations past saying such a thing? They wouldn't because parents simply expected their kids to contribute, rather than fanning them and feeding them grapes. It's been a cultural norm since Adam and Eve.

What's the solution? How about some Biblical wisdom that's just as useful today as it was 3,000 years ago? Proverbs 29:21 says: "If a man pampers his servant from youth, he will bring grief in the end" (NIV). Another translation says the slave will become "arrogant" (HCSB). Now, kids aren't exactly "servants" or "slave" in this sense of the word, but the principle applies just the same. Pampered kids are ungrateful kids and ungrateful kids are unhelpful kids. As the Proverb predicts, they "bring grief in the end" and become "arrogant"—sassy and self-centered. Just ask the beleaguered mom quoted in the paper or the one in aisle five with the back-talking bundle of joy.

If there's been a little too much pampering in your household, choose today to change that. You're the parent; you're in charge. Find a way to strike a more appropriate balance between your kids' rights and responsibilities. A start might be to adopt the old parenting adage "say yes when you can and no when you must." Trust me, when you say no, they'll get over it.

It may also be time to stop rationalizing and excusing their lack of assistance. Instead, assign real responsibilities to your kids and expect them to fulfill these responsibilities. Hold them accountable to help out. Successful household management, as well as successful parenting, avoids pampering and requires kids to carry their share of the load.

And remember, it's okay if your kids cry about getting fewer things, about being less entertained, about having to eat broccoli, or about your new responsibility policy. Kids need to cry every now and then. In fact, kids whose upbringing never causes them to cry usually end up making a lot of other people cry later on in life. They "bring grief in the end." So do yourself a favor—and do your kids a favor. Pamper them less and work them more. Then, you'll be amazed how much more time and energy you have to enjoy them.

Think About It

Is your household more kid-centered or more parent-centered? In other words, what usually drives the decisions about what you do and when you do it—the kids' desires or the parents' desires?

If it's the former, why are the kids in charge?

For Group Discussion

Consider the parenting guidance: "Say yes when you can and no when you must." It's easy to go too far in one direction or the other, especially when making adjustments to your parenting style. How can you maintain a proper balance, so that you're not saying yes too often or no too often?

Talk to God About It

Reflect on the Scripture "If a man pampers his servant from youth, he will bring grief in the end" (Prov. 29:21). When have you seen this proverbial wisdom in operation in your life?

Ask God to help you love your children without "pampering" them and for the discernment to set appropriate boundaries for them.

Your Freedom from Busyness Plan, Part 9

If you think your life may revolve too much around keeping your kids happy, then it surely does. What household chores and other responsibilities could be shifted to your kids? Start a list here and include the names of your children who will be assigned these responsibilities.

Study 10
Say No to TV

The man who had received five talents approached, presented five more talents, and said, "Master, you gave me five talents. Look, I've earned five more talents." Matthew 25:20

Imagine having an extra three hours a day, everyday. And you get to choose how you want to use it. Wouldn't that be great? How much more space would you have in your life to get things done? How much less hurried would you be because of the added time? How would three more hours a day affect your busyness problem?

Three extra hours a day. That's twenty-one extra hours a week, and more than a thousand extra hours a year. What would you do if God miraculously blessed you with this time, no strings attached?

If you're like the typical American, you won't need a miracle to claim this remarkable blessing. Just a new habit: the habit of saying no to TV.

Three hours a day is the approximate amount of television watched by the average adult in the United States, according to the most comprehensive study of time use ever conducted. In 2003, the U.S. Department of Labor interviewed more than twenty thousand people to uncover where we invest our time.[1] And of the fifteen and a half hours we spend awake each day, three of them—almost one-fifth of our waking hours—are devoted to TV watching.

The numbers vary a bit by gender (men watch a little more than women) and by age (people in their 20s and 30s watch TV about two hours a day; those in their 60s watch about four hours a day), but however you slice the data, these are sobering statistics. If how we spend our time is a measure of our priorities, then TV watching has become a higher priority than our relationships with those in our household, as well as our relationship with God.

It's remarkable that in a culture marked by hurry, busyness and overloaded schedules we somehow find the time to squeeze in a thousand hours of TV each year. Perhaps, though, it would be more accurate to turn this around—*because* we invest a thousand hours a year in our TV addiction, the rest of our lives are marked by hurry, busyness and overloaded schedules to get everything else done.

This is exclusively a contemporary problem. One reason that people throughout history have been less busy than we are today is because they didn't have television to drain their time. For us, though, short of ditching the TV altogether, there's no avoiding this temptation. So the solution is to trade the remote control for some self-control. To exercise restraint. To put ourselves on a TV diet and to create a new habit of spending our time in more meaningful ways.

That'll take discipline at first; maybe even some accountability until you form new habits. But the bottom line is that at its core, this is a choice. No one needs three hours a day—or even three minutes a day—of television to survive. God graciously permits us to choose how we'll steward the time He gives us.

Personally, I don't think solving the problem requires that we get rid of our TVs. Quite the contrary, occasionally, there's stuff worth watching, and TV can be a relaxing leisure activity. It's wise to consider, though, the linkage between our television and our busyness. How could your life be different if you had an additional three hours a day, an additional twenty-one hours a week, and an additional thousand hours a year?

Think About It

How much television do you watch on an average weekday?
How about on an average Saturday or Sunday?

If you do the math, about how much time does this amount to over the course of a year?

For Group Discussion

Jot down the television programs you watch regularly.

If Jesus sat down on the couch next to you while you were watching any of these, would you change the channel?

Talk to God About It

Reflect on the concept of stewardship—the theology that God owns everything and we are to manage (i.e., "steward") God's property in a way that honors Him. Normally, we think of stewardship as applying to how we use our money or our gifts and abilities. But it also applies to how we use our time. Ask God how much of your television watching is good stewardship.

Your Freedom from Busyness Plan, Part 10

If you cut your television watching in half, how much time would you reclaim?

How much more time might you reclaim if you also cut in half things like your recreational use of the Internet or your playing of video games?

If you do reclaim all this time, what's your plan for the use of the extra time?

---

[1] "American Time Use Survey—Table 1.," U.S. Department of Labor, Bureau of Labor Statistics, Washington DC, 12 January 2005 [cited 13 September 2005]. Available from the Internet: *www.bls.gov/news.release/atus.toc.htm.*

Fast is the Enemy of Love

But a Samaritan on his journey came up to him, and when he saw [the man], he had compassion. He went over to him and bandaged his wounds, pouring on oil and wine. Then he put him on his own animal, brought him to an inn, and took care of him. Luke 10:33-34

You've seen the scene, perhaps even experienced it close up like I did. There I was, driving down the road, prudence personified behind the wheel. All of a sudden some product of the me-first culture comes flying out of a gas station and cuts me off, barely missing my bumper. I hit the brakes, but not the horn. Honking displeases God, you know. But then I notice something else displeasing. On the back of the minivan that just cut me off was a little fish—the universal symbol of a born-again on board. The outward sign of an inward reality. This driver's a Christian and is boldly proclaiming that to the world—or at least the world behind his four-wheeled weapon.

Normally, it's a great thing to profess fearlessly what we believe. We need much more of that among believers. When we're marring the cause of Christ because of our hurry, though, some things are better left unprofessed.

We see similar speed-induced setbacks around the neighborhood when, for the sake of time, we avoid those who live next door. Who has time for small talk these days, much less a barbecue? We see the problem in our homes, as we trade efficiency for quality time with our kids. "Pick a shorter book for Daddy to read," we say at bedtime, keeping one eye on the clock so we don't miss some TV show. In the workplace, it's arguably even worse. How many times do we rush past others' needs, offering no more than a quick, indifferent "hello" to them, because we're so focused on getting the next thing done?

For many of us Christians who are rushing through life, the salt shaker ran out of granules years ago. And that's tragic. When our interaction with others says: "I have something more important to do," they feel the same way that I felt when I was cut off by that little fish. "What a hypocrite!" they might think. "Where's the compassion? Where's the love? What's with the 'me-first' attitude?" It's enough to make them want to lean on their horn.

It's been said quite correctly that "you'll meet more spiritually needy people than your pastor ever will" and that "your life is the only Bible many people will ever read." Those aren't bumper sticker clichés, they're realities. Ours is an awesome, *awesome* responsibility. If the New Testament is to be believed, other people's very eternity may be affected by how we conduct ourselves in our daily lives! Do we really need another reason to slow down and take seriously our roles as ambassadors of the faith?

The time may be right for you to turn a corner on this issue. To find out, take inventory of yourself during the next two or three days. Look for signs that your hurry is compromising your witness. Consider this at the most telling moments, like immediately after conversations or at the end of your commute or in a time of sincere reflection at the end of the day. Examine yourself through the eyes of those around you. Do you need to alter your pace of life?

Fast is the enemy of love. We can't love people in a hurry. We can't serve them in a hurry, listen to them in a hurry, empathize or comfort them in a hurry. They'll see that we're just going through the motions of our faith, and it may in fact drive them further away from God.

So slow down. A lot more than your bumper is at stake.

Think About It

Consider how the pace of your life is affecting others and then write your conclusions in the space provided.

Does God want you to alter your pace of life?

For Group Discussion

In what situations is hurry adversely affecting your relationships and/or your witness? Or think about it this way: *If Jesus were you for one day, with what activities would he take more time?*

Talk to God About It

Read (slowly) and reflect on the parable of the Good Samaritan (Luke 10:30-37). Ask God when in recent days you have been like the priest, and in what situations He wants you to be more like the Samaritan.

Your Freedom from Busyness Plan, Part 11

What is the one area where you will make significant progress slowing down this month?

How will you make sure this happens?

God Wants You to Rest

For the LORD made the heavens and the earth, the sea, and everything in them in six days; then He rested on the seventh day. Therefore the LORD blessed the Sabbath day and declared it holy. Exodus 20:11

We know we shouldn't, but we do anyway. And it's not a little problem. Among Christians, five out of ten men and six out of ten women say they "sometimes," "often," or "always" feel guilty when they relax.[1]

According to the data, it's not much of an issue during our teenage years, but the problem grows through our twenties, peaks in our thirties, and only gradually declines through our forties and fifties. By our sixties, we're not much better at guilt-free rest than we were three decades earlier.

As we saw in Study 1, there's evidence that an epidemic of busyness has infected the body of Christ. Our guilt about relaxing is a sure symptom, as well as a contributing cause. If rest makes us feel guilty, we'll get less rest than we should.

For many of us, the unfortunate reality is that guilt is the motor that drives our daily overload. But did you ever consider God's perspective on rest and relaxation?

Well, for starters, He invented it. "The seventh day is a Sabbath to the Lord your God. You must not do any work" (Ex. 20:10). I know you know that, but has the theology migrated from your head to your heart? One way to tell is by what you do on the Sabbath. Do your activities on that day line up with God's will for that day? Another way to tell is how invigorated you feel because of the Sabbath. Are you rejuvenated the morning after?

As Jesus said, "The Sabbath was made for man and not man for the Sabbath" (Mark 2:27). It's a special gift God gives to us each week. How often we leave that gift wrapped and sitting in a corner!

When our Sabbath looks similar to the other six days, that's leaving the gift wrapped. And when we fill it up with a lot of activity or with work, that's leaving the gift wrapped. Instead, God wants us to be refreshed by our Sabbath. That's part of what He's put in the box. We should feel no more guilty about accepting that refreshment than we should about opening a present.

There's another reason we shouldn't feel guilty when we relax. Adequate rest is essential to real progress in the Christian life. You may know this first-hand. Without adequate rest, we tend to engage spiritual disciplines like prayer, worship, Bible reading, and growth group meetings as "one more thing to do." When not done in a spirit of joy and expectation, they lose their power to change us.

Professor Dallas Willard, one of today's most eloquent authorities on spiritual formation, puts it this way:

> Bible study, prayer and church attendance, among the most commonly prescribed activities in Christian circles, generally have little effect for soul transformation, as is obvious to any observer. ... Their failure to bring about change is precisely because the body and soul are so exhausted, fragmented and conflicted that the prescribed activities cannot be appropriately engaged, and by and large degenerate into legalistic and ineffectual rituals.
>
> ...God will, generally speaking, not compete for our attention. If we will not withdraw from things that obsess and exhaust us into solitude and silence, he will usually leave us to our own devices.[2]

Notice the paradox: slowing down can speed up our spiritual growth. Rest is part of God's design for a healthy spiritual life, not just a healthy physical and emotional life. So when we deprive ourselves of adequate rest, living a life of hurry and overload, we are actually separating ourselves from God's will. It's all the more lamentable, then, that so many of us Christians say "I feel guilty when I relax." In fact, the opposite should be true. We should safeguard rest and if necessary, schedule times of rest—daily breaks, a weekly Sabbath, a quarterly or annual retreat for spiritual renewal—in full confidence that this is what God wants us to do. To rest is not to be lazy. From God's perspective, rest is a holy activity.

Remember that it's a gift as well. God is inviting you to relax more, guilt-free. This week and this next Sabbath, will you finally unwrap and enjoy His gift?

Think About It

Guilt about rest is a trap that inhibits our holiness. How often do you fall into it?

For Group Discussion

What does your typical Sabbath look like and how rested do you feel at the beginning of the next day?

What are some activities that might be better left for another day?

Talk to God About It

"Good Sabbaths make good Christians," as the Puritans used to say, because they draw us closer to God and provide respite necessary to love God and love others all week long. We can extend that Puritanical wisdom, based on Dallas Willard's insight, and say that "good rest makes good Christians." Talk to God about how much "good rest" you get and ask Him how much more He wants you to get.

Your Freedom from Busyness Plan, Part 12

What's your plan for carving out more time for rest? What needs to change in your life so you can schedule significant times of personal retreat daily, weekly and annually?

---

[1]These statistics were generated using the same dataset of 13,000 Christians mentioned in Study 1 of this book.
[2]Willard, Dallas: "Spiritual Disciplines, Spiritual Formation, and the Restoration of the Soul," *Journal of Psychology and Theology*, Volume 26, Number 1 (La Mirada, CA: Rosemead School of Psychology-Biola University, Spring 1998), 107.

Minimize Multitasking and Live in the Moment

What is your life? You are a mist that appears for a little while and then vanishes. James 4:14, NIV

The busyness of modern life has transformed us into a culture of multitaskers. It may seem innocuous enough—after all, we're just getting more done with the limited amount of time available to us—but as we'll see in a minute, multitasking comes with an exorbitant price tag.

Sometimes multitasking is unavoidable. Just ask any harried mom who has to watch a toddler or two and prepare a meal at the same time. But it's also the case that we're willing accomplices to much of our multitasking. Do any of these situations sound familiar? You're on the phone but sending an e-mail simultaneously. You're listening to your spouse but thinking about something else you have to do. You're hearing your child's account of his day but also scanning the headlines in the paper. You're driving and eating a burger while talking on the cell phone.

We rationalize that it has to be this way to satisfy all our responsibilities. Consider this, though: there's a growing body of evidence from psychologists and brain researchers (especially out of the University of Michigan, Harvard, and Carnegie Mellon University) indicating that not only do we perform our tasks more poorly when we multitask, habitual multitasking also culminates in greater stress and in short-term memory loss.[3]

Maybe that explains why you have trouble recalling some of your day when someone asks you at dinnertime how your day went. Maybe that also explains why you sometimes walk into a room of your house, looking to retrieve something, but when you get to that room you've forgotten what it was you were looking for. You stand there in the middle of the room, dumbfounded, racking your brain for the reason you're there. But you were so busy mentally multitasking that en route, you lost one of the tasks.

Bottom line: "Multitasking makes you stupid" (to borrow a headline from media reports of these studies). Pretty amazing, huh? We expect bread and get a stone.

There's an even more important reason to minimize multitasking, though: when we do it, we shortchange people. Our spouse, our kids, our parents, our siblings, our coworkers, our friends ... usually, the people who eat the bitter fruit of our multitasking are those closest to us. Those God has entrusted to us. Because of our busy lives, for these people, too often we're there but not there.

Jesus knew better. He lived in the moment, focusing exclusively on the person before him, the situation at hand, the present. The woman at the well, the centurion, the disciples, the rich young man, the blind men, the lepers—they all had his complete attention. Read any Gospel story and you'll see that this is in fact true of every person with whom Jesus interacted, even those who interrupted what He was doing at the time.

Jesus wasn't so overloaded with things to do that He had to shortchange people. As a result, He modeled for us something God wants us to remember everyday: the most important person in the world is the person to whom you are talking. So don't multitask the moment away.

What would it take for you to embrace this lesson? What would it take to discipline your thought life so you could live in the moment and give people your complete, undivided attention? How much less stressful would your life be if you focused on one thing at a time? How much better would your relationships be if you did?

And most importantly, how much more would people see Jesus in you?

Think About It
Assume you were going to try to minimize your multitasking. List the positive and negative consequences of this change. Do the positives outweigh the negatives?

For Group Discussion
What would it take for you to discipline your thought life so you could live in the moment and give people your complete, undivided attention?

How much less stressful would your life be if you focused on one thing at a time?

How much better would your relationships be if you did?

And how much more would people see Jesus in you?

Talk to God About It
Ask God to show you whom you shortchange by being "there but not there" for them. Ask God to help you be fully present to live in the moment with them.

Your Freedom from Busyness Plan, Part 13
Today, tell someone who knows you well that you're trying to reduce your multi-tasking and to live in the moment. Ask this person to touch base with you once a day for the next seven days to ask how you did that day with your commitment.

---

[3]Sue Shellenbarger, "Multitasking Makes You Stupid: Studies Show Pitfalls of Doing Too Much at Once," *The Wall Street Journal*, February 27, 2003, D1.

Reframe Your Prayer Life

Rejoice always! Pray constantly. Give thanks in everything, for this is God's will for you in Christ Jesus. 1 Thessalonians 5:16-18

"How's your prayer life?"

It's been said that this is one of the two questions that make Christians most uncomfortable (the other question is "Have you led anyone to Christ lately?") One of the problems with our prayer life is that it's something we always intend to get to when we've finished everything else. Many of us are simply too busy to pray and when we do, we're tired or distracted. God gets the crumbs of our day, so why should it surprise us that our relationship with Him is crummy?

One way some people have tried to get around this problem is to schedule time for the relationship—to engage God at particular times and places, like mealtime, bedtime, Sunday worship time, and so forth. This approach, of course, has the advantage of ensuring that we do spend some time communicating with God each day, so He's not crowded out of our lives entirely. But the approach can suffer from a fatal flaw: When our relationship with God is relegated to specific times and places, the relationship can become intermittent. We compartmentalize God, rather than making Him our constant companion. Not exactly the biblical ideal.

Despite our busy schedules, there's a better way to a healthy prayer life. Start by recognizing the longstanding distinction between saying prayers and prayer, and embrace both. Saying prayers is what we do before a meal or beside a hospital bed or corporately with a Sunday school class, but prayer has nothing to do with saying anything, aloud or silently. Rather, prayer is simply a mindfulness of God in whatever we're doing—a sensitivity to God's presence, moment to moment throughout our day. It's "practicing the presence of God" in everything we do, to use a poignant term coined by Brother Lawrence in the seventeenth century.

The idea far predates the seventeenth century, though. When the Apostle Paul instructed the Thessalonian church to "pray constantly" (1 Thess. 5:17), he was encouraging prayer, not saying prayers. He was not teaching that God wants us to remain on our knees perpetually; rather, he was teaching that God invites us to go about our daily affairs in continual mindfulness of Him.

Think about it: What else could "pray constantly" possibly mean except to be mindful of God constantly? We learn this lesson from the life of Jesus. Indeed, Jesus often went off by Himself to pray, yet His whole life was prayer since He was continually mindful of His Father. This is the model for our prayer life as well.

Notice that this is a complete reframing of prayer. It means that reading this study, as you are right now, can be prayer if you're mindful of God as you are doing it. It means that working at your job can be prayer, if you are keeping God in mind as you work. Similarly, doing housework can be prayer, driving can be prayer, schoolwork can be prayer, answering an e-mail can be prayer, disciplining a child can be prayer, being intimate with your spouse can be prayer, exercising can be prayer. The most ordinary of activities—even simply drinking a glass of water— can be prayer. Paul told the Corinthians, "Whether you eat or drink, or whatever you do, do everything for God's glory" (1 Cor. 10:31).

Get it? Whether something is prayer depends on whether we're cognizant of God while we're doing it. When we're God-conscious, we're in a state of prayerfulness. That's what God desires for our prayer life, not long-winded, eloquent prayer speeches that we make publicly and privately (Matt. 6:7).

Notice that this reframing of prayer as mindfulness also dispenses forever with our tendency to be a "checklist Christian." The more mindful we become of God in our daily activities, the more that everything on our to-do list becomes a spiritual activity. "Time with God" moves from being an item on the list to being everything on the list.

Reframe your prayer life. See prayer as mindfulness, not speaking. If you make this adjustment, you'll never again have to feel guilty about being too busy for prayer.

Think About It

If you're like many Christians, your prayer life is not what you want it to be. Write down three words that describe your prayer life today, and three words that describe what you'd like your prayer life to be one month from now.

For Group Discussion

Prayer is different from saying prayers. We can think of prayer as mindfulness of God or being God-conscious. How God-conscious are you in a typical day?

What could you do to become more God-conscious in everything you do—to move toward the New Testament ideal of praying constantly?

Talk to God About It

Scripture says that in everything we do, we should be mindful of God. Take a few minutes to think through the activities of your typical day, and ask God, after reflecting on each activity, to help you transform this activity into prayer.

Your Freedom from Busyness Plan, Part 14

Write down some ideas for how you will evaluate your mindfulness of God—that is, your prayer life—on a daily basis.

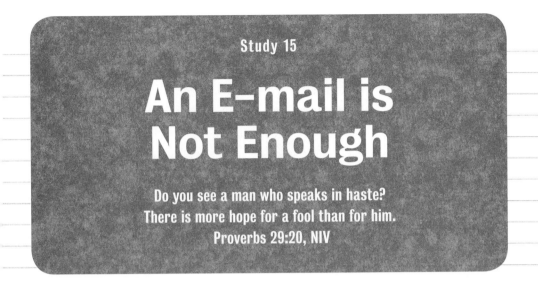

An E-mail is Not Enough

**Do you see a man who speaks in haste?
There is more hope for a fool than for him.
Proverbs 29:20, NIV**

What if Esther just sent an e-mail? Forget the royal robes. Forget the subtle strut. Forget the elaborate dinners. This job needed to be done fast, so she just sent a quick missive to try to save the day. "Honey. That Haman creep is plotting to kill all my brothers and sisters. Don't listen to him. Love, E." Do you think the outcome would have been the same?

What if Nehemiah just sent an e-mail? Instead of waiting months for God's timing, he simply pointed and clicked: "Dear King Art, I'd like to request a sabbatical from my cupbearer job so that I can build a wall. Time is of the essence. Please respond by close of business today." Do you think the king would have been as amenable to his request?

How about Moses? What if this busy guy just sent a bunch of e-mails to Pharaoh so he could get back to his family and his sheep? "Rameses: This is to inform you that I Am says you ain't. So let His people go or else." He could have even decorated the electronic messages with some animation—staffs that turn into snakes, perhaps. Would Pharaoh have even opened the junk mail?

What if Paul just sent e-mails? Certainly he was a prolific writer, so maybe it would have been more efficient to simply stay in Damascus and spend his days mass-mailing the Gentile world. His words would have reached a lot more of them, but would he really have reached any?

And what if Jesus just sent an e-mail? "Dear children of Israel, Please visit my Web site, *PowerfulParables.com*. Life changing stuff there." Surely that would have been a lot faster than roaming the countryside teaching them in small groups. Do you think He would have captured their hearts?

We live in a world of instant, electronic communications. That's a tremendous blessing, from a kingdom perspective. Without ever setting foot outside of our homes, we have the potential to teach people, encourage people, and to even change lives across town or across the planet. Double click, write, send. Off goes a letter to China. Point, click, build a home page. Look mom, I have my own web-ministry to support missionaries! Such opportunities were unthinkable to 99.9 percent of the people who ever walked this earth, and they are truly opportunities from God.

Technology offers expedient tools. Highly efficient tools. But the trade-off is that they're also highly impersonal tools. For those of us in that habit of hurry, e-mail and similar technologies allow us to manage and maintain relationships at arms-length, whether with relatives, friends, coworkers, or others. Sometimes that erodes rather than erects relationships.

Have you experienced this? If you use e-mail, my guess is that you know exactly what I'm talking about. Who among us hasn't been on the receiving end of a terse e-mail, when a phone call or personal visit would have been more appropriate? Recently I got one that said something like "M — Sorry about my comment in the meeting. My bad. Won't happen again. — C." A note like that is one step forward, two steps back.

Don't be too busy to be personal. Consider how you use the technologies of our day and whether you're overusing them for the sake of fast. If so, make a commitment to pick up the phone more often ... and to visit in person more often. Important relationships take time and are worth the additional effort.

That was God's approach. Think about it. What if God, because He was in a hurry to save us, just sent us an e-mail instead of sending His Son? Do you think you'd be reading this book today?

Think About It

This study encourages the following: "Consider how you use the technologies of our day and whether you're overusing them for the sake of fast." This is an issue that's only going to get worse over time, as technological advances make it even easier to relate to people at arm's length. In what situations do you send an e-mail when you should communicate more personally?

For Group Discussion

E-mail, instant messaging, and other electronic media can be wonderful tools when used with discretion. But as indicated in this study, they can also adversely affect our relationships. How, if at all, have your relationships been adversely affected by electronic communications?

Talk to God About It

Reflect on the proverb: "Do you see a man who speaks in haste? There is more hope for a fool than for him" (Prov. 29:20, NIV). As we sometimes find out the hard way, electronic communications make us even more susceptible to speaking "in haste." Take a few minutes and ask God to help you use the blessings of technology in a way that strengthens rather than weakens your relationships.

Your Freedom from Busyness Plan, Part 15

Look at your answer to the "Think About It" question above. What's your plan to ensure that you won't use e-mail in situations when you should be speaking personally with someone?

The Blessing of a Simpler Life, Part 1

He said to him, "Love the Lord your God with all your heart,
with all your soul, and with all your mind.
This is the greatest and most important commandment. The second
is like it: Love your neighbor as yourself. Matthew 22: 37-39

The simple life is the life God intends for us. The busy life is the life our culture conditions us to accept instead.

God's invitation to simplicity stands, though, regardless of how hectic your life has become and regardless what you've obligated yourself to do or to pay for. Want some encouragement? Here are a dozen snapshots of your future if you RSVP to His invitation with a "yes."

When you embrace simpler living
- your calendar will have a lot more white space than color;
- you'll be able to work fewer hours, because you have fewer bills to pay because you've learned to live with fewer things;
- you'll be able to take a walk, not for exercise or for the dog, but because you have the time to take a walk. And you'll recognize God's graces during that walk, rather than using the time to mentally get things done;
- you'll get ready in the morning without concern for what people will think of your clothes, your hair, or your body;
- you'll be able to wait in a line of people or cars without instinctively looking at your watch;
- you'll savor every bite of the meal in gratitude, instead of gulping it down as usual;

- you'll step off the treadmill of career climbing and professional legacy, and instead you'll do something you love;
- you'll be able to pray in front of people, but talk only to God;
- you'll focus on one thing at a time—living in the moment without concern about what's not getting done;
- you'll look at a pile of laundry or dishes or at a cluttered closet and sincerely thank God for the abundance of your life;
- you'll have the strength to say no even though the sign says "sale";
- you'll be content with the blessings in your life ... finally.

Sound like a step forward from the life you have now? It very well may be, because God didn't design us to live hyper-complicated lives, encumbered with obligations or possessions or other things that distract us from what matters most. He designed us, as Jesus said, to have the time and the space to love Him and love others (Matthew 22:37-39). If you're looking for an authoritative answer to the timeless question "How shall we live," Jesus offers it with ... well ... simplicity.

But recognize something else essential about this simpler lifestyle. Retreating to it does not begin with changing the externals of our life—our debt level, our spending habits, the number of activities we agree to undertake, the speed we drive, and so forth. Try to make progress that way and you'll become a Pharisee in no time. Instead, a simpler life begins with internal transformation; it's the fruit of an inner life that's centered on God—an inner life that empowers us to see as He sees and thereby to live as He invites us to live. In the words of Richard Foster, "simplicity is an inward reality that can be seen in an outward lifestyle."[1]

So, connecting the dots, the theology is this: beating busyness flows from adopting a simpler lifestyle which flows from genuine God-centeredness. How can we gain this divine center, this fresh and liberating perspective, once and for all? And how can we resist the ever-present cultural currents that push us back toward our old priorities? These are critical questions—questions that we'll address in the rest of this week's studies.

Think About It

What's the first thing that comes to mind when you hear the term "a simple lifestyle"?

Do you think it means to live like the Amish?

Do you think it means trading your car for a bike and your laptop for an abacus?

Do you think it means giving up steak and potatoes for tofu and alfalfa sprouts?

These and other misconceptions lead Christians to reject the potential of simplicity. What might you do to better understand what "a simple lifestyle" really means from God's perspective?

For Group Discussion

Look over the simplicity list on pages 57-58. How many of these items describe you?

And what does your answer tell you about the potential for improvement in your life?

Talk to God About It

Take a few minutes to meditate on whether your life really has a "divine center" to it? Ask God during this time what, if anything, is the connection between a deficit in your God-centeredness and the busyness and overload of your life.

Your Freedom from Busyness Plan, Part 16

What are three things in your life that need to change if you want to accept God's invitation to live a simpler life?

How will you ensure that these things change?

[1] Richard J. Foster, *Freedom of Simplicity*, (HarperCollins: San Francisco, 1981), 8.

The Blessing of a Simpler Life, Part 2

Do not be conformed to this age, but be transformed by the renewing of your mind, so that you may discern what is the good, pleasing, and perfect will of God. Romans 12:2

Do you know a Joe and Tanya? Those are names I made up for a couple I know that was stressed out from their "toxic work-and-spend" cycle. A couple who worked too much to buy too much, but didn't see one another too much. Well, let me tell you the rest of their story.

Last year they decided to splurge for a getaway to Brazil. The travel brochures were incredible, boasting of a country so abundant in beautiful weather, beautiful countryside and beautiful people that its citizens gratefully proclaim "God is Brazilian." The trip was a stretch for their budget, but it seemed too good to pass up.

But as they flew into Sao Paulo, an enormous city with three times the population of Los Angeles and twice the area of Rhode Island, what they saw belied the brochures. Sao Paulo was a carpet of poverty. Thousands of square miles of squalor—literally thousands. From 2,000 feet up, they viewed the countless *favelas*—the slums—and they extended as far as the eye could see.

The image haunted Joe and Tanya—enough so that they altered some of their vacation plans. Their taxi driver, Rodolfo, served as an impromptu tour guide. He told them that poverty is a way of life in the city, that unemployment and crime are everywhere, and that the police have even abandoned many neighborhoods because of the violence. But the worst part was the children—skinny, vivacious children of all ages populating every alley and corner. Rodolfo explained some of them have families, but many are orphans.

"They're street children," he said. "The street is their home. Some try to make money as roving vendors, some just beg. Many, though, sell drugs, weapons, or even their bodies just so they can eat. Why not? they figure. Because of hunger and disease and murder, many of the kids don't expect to make it until adulthood anyway."

Joe and Tanya were stunned. What Rodolfo revealed in broken English broke their hearts. God had blessed them with so much, and they returned to Him so little. How could they have been so blind? How could they have thought that possessions, comfort and career were so important, when so many in the world are barely surviving? One thing was for sure: their life would never be the same.

Through this experience, God transformed the lives of Joe and Tanya, shepherding them to a life of non-negotiable priorities: God first, quality time with family, faithful stewardship of income, and simplicity in everything. Perspective on the blessings in their life yielded gratitude and gratitude yielded contentment. Contentment, in turn, permitted them to live a simpler life of less work, less spending, less running around—less overload. Their new reality of gratitude to God yielded a lifestyle of simplicity. The weight of busyness lifted from their lives.

Today, to help them maintain perspective, Joe and Tanya keep a picture of Sao Paulo on their wall. And they're returning to that city again soon—this time on a missions trip to minister to street children.

God used their escape to Brazil to help them escape from bondage. He blessed them with a perspective that cured their blindness and ultimately, their busyness.

And He wants to do the same for you. He continues to invite you to gain a perspective—a new way of thinking—that will help you live more simply. The formal invitation reads: "Do not conform any longer to the pattern of this world, but be transformed by the renewing of your mind" (Rom. 12:2, NIV).

"Cultural currents" threaten to drown out our context of abundance and carry us back to our old patterns of thinking and living. If you want to live a simpler life, God says seek a renewed mind. Like Joe and Tanya, the more you focus on how blessed you are rather than on what's missing from your life, the more you can enjoy the blessing of a simpler life. Perspective is power.

Think About It
On the surface, today's study may have seemed only remotely connected to beating busyness, but it digs down to a root cause and offers a permanent solution. What was the root cause of the couple's over-extended life and why are they unlikely to return to that life?

For Group Discussion
When you think about the quality of your life, what's your benchmark? In other words, against what or whom do you measure your quality of life?

No matter what we have, we tend not to see our life as terribly abundant. But what if our benchmark were a single parent in a Brazilian slum, or a refugee in the Sudan, or a homeless person in the next city? How would that frame of reference change your thinking and your ability to live a simpler life?

Talk to God About It
Reflect on Romans 12:2: "Do not conform any longer to the pattern of this world, but be transformed by the renewing of your mind." Ask God to reveal to you the greatest threats to gaining a renewed mind—a mind that focuses on how blessed you are and that avoids thinking about what's still missing from your life.

Your Freedom from Busyness Plan, Part 17
Joe and Tanya thought it critical to hang a picture of Sao Paulo on their wall to keep perspective. What daily reminders will you keep before you of the abundance of your life?

The Obstacle of Overspending

Do not love the world or the things that belong to the world.
If anyone loves the world, love for the Father is not in him.
Because everything that belongs to the world—the lust of the flesh,
the lust of the eyes, and the pride in one's lifestyle—is not from
the Father, but is from the world. 1 John 2:15-16

Warning: Marketers know you better than you know yourself.

You might find that hard to believe, but in all likelihood, it's true. Promotion and sales have become more science than art in recent decades, leaving us more transparent than we ever thought we'd be. Market researchers in companies and universities have invested literally billions of dollars to understand consumer behavior—to know what leads you to buy something or to walk away—and that research has yielded remarkably sophisticated tactics to separate people from their money. Take it from a business professor: these people are data-driven geniuses.

On one hand this is not a bad thing, since it makes our companies more competitive and keeps people employed. In fact, if marketers and salespeople didn't enjoy some success, none of us would have jobs!

But on the other hand, their fascinating science of persuasion has also helped create a culture of consumerism—a habit of discontent that engenders a habit of continually seeking more. Just look at all the recreational shopping we do, our delight when a new catalog shows up in the mail, the accumulation of stuff in our attics, basements, closets, cabinets, and garages ... not to mention our credit card debt, our hefty car loans, and our bloated mortgages. It all points to a life-style of overspending.

In fairness, sophisticated marketing is not the only culprit here. Many of us, without anyone's help, have come to worship gods like comfort, convenience and comparison—gods that ordain our overspending. We suffer from "the lust of the eyes" for worldly things, as John puts it (1 John 2:16), so if we are victims of brilliant marketers, we are sometimes willing victims.

Now, what does all this have to do with busyness? The connections are not hard to discern. One connection is that our habit of purchasing luxuries amounts to almost a part-time job. We invest a lot of time shopping for the best prices and making purchases, as well as maintaining, fixing, and replacing all these things.

A second connection to busyness is that our habits of spending and accumulation require that we work more to keep up with the bills. Many people work far too many hours, because they've become trapped in the "work-and-spend cycle" I've mentioned earlier this week. Some people genuinely desire to reduce their work hours or take a less taxing, lower paying job—they want to live a simpler life—but they can't because of their financial obligations. They're trapped (or so they think) working in jobs that are little more than "golden handcuffs." Their good job simultaneously enables them and enslaves them.

If anything that's been said here looks like the person you see in the mirror, let me suggest that you pick up two shields to defend yourself. First, equip yourself with the shield of sensitivity. Be sensitive to the fact that there are lots of people out there shrewdly enticing you to overspend. Be aware that you're vulnerable to the powerful current of slick marketing. It can subtly lure you in to the cult of consumerism. Watch for it and don't be duped into buying things you don't need.

Second, and more importantly, equip yourself with the shield of stewardship. We touched on the concept back in Week 2 when discussing appropriate use of our time. It's every bit as applicable here, when discussing use of our money. That's because it's God's money, and we're just stewarding it for Him. Do you think of it that way with every purchase? The more you can remember that the dollars are His, the more likely you'll be to spend wisely—to be content with what God has given you and to enjoy the blessings of a simpler life.

Overspending increases overload. Stewardship increases simplicity.

Think About It

How much of the busyness and complexity of your life is a result of shopping for, purchasing, returning and maintaining luxury items (i.e., items that you don't need to survive)?

For Group Discussion

How often do you think about the issue of stewardship when you're spending money?

What could you do to maintain a stewardship mindset all the time?

Talk to God About It

Reflect on 1 John 2:15-17: "Do not love the world or the things that belong to the world. If anyone loves the world, love for the Father is not in him. Because every-thing that belongs to the world—the lust of the flesh, the lust of the eyes, and the pride in one's lifestyle—is not from the Father, but is from the world. And the world with its lust is passing away, but the one who does God's will remains forever." Take a few minutes and ask God to show you whether you have a problem with "the lust of the flesh" or "the lust of the eyes"—cravings for worldly things. Ask Him whether He wants you to make any adjustments with regard to your spending.

Your Freedom from Busyness Plan, Part 18

If God is asking you to scale back your purchases and to be a better steward of His money, identify three things you will do in the coming weeks to faithfully comply with His wishes.

The Obstacle of Overwork

The LORD God took the man and placed him in the garden of Eden to work it and watch over it. Genesis 2:15

"Sir, did I hear you right?" asked the senator. "Did you say by 1985 Americans will be working twenty-two hours a week? And working only twenty-seven weeks of the year? And retiring at age 38? Is that your estimate?"

"That's right," the witness responded, still in disbelief that he was actually testifying before a Congressional committee. "Personally, senator, our biggest problem in the future will be figuring out what to do with all our free time!"[2]

Laughable? Certainly in retrospect. But in 1967, experts testified to these predictions before Congress. The reality is that by the mid 1980s, the average American was working about 41 hours a week for 47 weeks a year, about 163 hours more than in the late 1960s.[3] And today, our work hours per year in the United States are even higher, exceeding those of every other industrialized country. As a result, God time, family time, rest, recreation, volunteering, and just about everything else that matters in life has been squeezed.

It's not that being industrious is a bad thing; it's just that for many of us, our work hours are now far out of proportion with the other things that God desires for us. Some reasons we voluntarily work too much include our ambition, our desire to impress others, our love for our work—even our belief that our worth depends on our position and paycheck.

Then there's the number one *involuntary* reason that many of us work too much. A new world of global competition has led many organizations to require more hours from each employee. Long hours have become the norm in many workplaces, so there's usually no way to avoid overwork for those employed there. There are solutions to the problem, though. Let me suggest a few from my experience.

I've spent a lot of time teaching and counseling adult Christians, as well as researching Christians' lifestyles. What I've concluded is that for many of these people, to live the life God wants them to live will require them to find other work that entails fewer hours. For some, that work could be in the same organization, or even a scaled-back version of their current job. But for many others, it would mean changing organizations or even changing careers. Their job is their obstacle to living the life God wants them to live.

If you can scale back your spending significantly, then you have the freedom to scale back the time you spend working, leaving more time for all those things you've been neglecting for years.

It's common sense. It's just uncommon practice.

It needn't be uncommon, though. Except for those just barely getting by on their current income, this comes down to a choice. God has blessed you with the ability to choose a quality life of modesty and simplicity, instead of exhausting overwork.

The cultural currents push us toward the latter. They encourage us to accept the lie that our self-worth is tied to what we earn, what we accomplish, and what position we hold. Buy-in to that assumption and you're at risk of becoming the workaholic you vowed you'd never be. In fact, you may already be there. If you want to know for sure, ask someone who will give it to you straight. Don't ask yourself.

Let's be clear about something: pursuing a simpler, higher quality life does not automatically mean stepping away from leadership or other positions of influence. It does not automatically mean giving up on your career or your dreams (but it may mean finally realizing those dreams.) It does mean, however, seeking God's will in earnest, discerning how much time He wants you to invest in work, and identifying what work He wants you to do—and then making adjustments to respond to His will.

Ultimately, God may not recommend that you retreat to a twenty-two hour work-week and buy a smaller house in the country ... or He may. But one thing's for sure: whatever God forecasts for your future will be a lot more reliable than what we're told in Congressional hearings.

So trust Him.

Think About It
If you work more hours than you'd like to work, identify at least three reasons for that. Think deeply before answering, trying to get to the root causes.

For Group Discussion
Being a workaholic, whether you're paid for your work or not, is one of the scourges of contemporary Christian life. Many Christians work too much. Do you? How do you know if you have a problem?

Talk to God About It
Genesis 2:15,18 says, "The Lord God took the man and placed him in the Garden of Eden to work it and watch over it. ... Then the Lord God said, 'It is not good for the man to be alone. I will make a helper who is like him.' " Adam got a job and a wedding ring within four verses of one another. Talk to God about this timeless struggle for balance in your current life and whether He wants it to be different.

Your Freedom from Busyness Plan, Part 19
What's your plan to evaluate whether God wants you to alter your work hours, your job, or your career? Whose advice will you seek to discern God's will?

---

[2]Paraphrased testimony from a 1967 Senate Subcommittee hearing, cited by Nancy Gibbs, "How America Has Run Out of Time," *Time*, Vol. 133, No. 17, 24 April 1989, 59.
[3]Julie B. Schor, *The Overworked American*, (Basic Books: New York, 1991), 30, 35.

Reorder Your Life Around God

"The Lᴏʀᴅ of Hosts says this: These people say:
The time has not come for the house of the Lᴏʀᴅ to be rebuilt."
The word of the Lᴏʀᴅ came through Haggai the prophet:
"Is it time for you yourselves to live in your paneled houses,
while this house lies in ruins?" Now the Lᴏʀᴅ of Hosts says this:
"Think carefully about your ways."   Haggai 1:2–5

There is an epidemic of busyness among Christians. And throughout this book we've seen that two of the consequences of our busyness are a compromised relationship with God and a lower quality of life.

Did you know, though, that these same problems have plagued God's people for thousands of years? That's how pervasive they've been. Twenty-five hundred years ago, for example, a prophet named Haggai delivered much the same message to the people of Israel. Makes you wonder when we're going to learn our lesson.

Haggai taught and wrote after the Babylonian exile. When many of the Israelites returned from captivity in about 538 B.C., they began rebuilding the temple that was destroyed decades earlier. But as of 520 B.C., when Haggai entered the scene, the temple still lay in ruins.

This is not a trivial matter since the temple wasn't just any building. And it wasn't just a place of worship and sacrifice. In Old Testament times, the temple was, first and foremost, a place for God to dwell among His people. He didn't dwell in the hearts of believers, as He does in the New Covenant. For God to be among and in relationship with His chosen, there needed to be a temple.

Consider, then, what is implied by a temple lying in ruins. Relationship with God is not a priority for these people. It's not even on the radar screen. Why is that? Haggai 1:2 and 1:4 tell us:

> The Lord of Hosts says this: "These people say: The time has not come for the house of the Lord to be rebuilt. ... Is it a time for you yourselves to live in your paneled houses, while this house lies in ruins?"

"Paneled houses"? At the time, a paneled house was an extravagantly built house—something that required a lot of time and effort to build. Something with multiple rooms, modeled in cedar. Something that takes significant resources to build and that one cares for meticulously.

God, through Haggai, strikingly called their attention to it: "Is it time for you yourselves to live in your paneled houses, while this house lies in ruins?"

Fast-forward 2,500 years, and ask yourself the same question: How's my relationship with God these days? What's my temple look like? Have I built it? Do I attend to it? Am I taking the time to maintain it? Or has my schedule relegated the development of my relationship with God to perpetual back-burner status? Is my temple of relationship with God a project that I'm always intending to get to, but for various reasons, I never quite get there?

If your temple is lying in ruins—if God is regularly crowded out of your life, like He was for the Israelites—then these consequences, described in Haggai 1:5-6,9 will probably resonate with you:

> Now this is what the Lord Almighty says: "Give careful thought to your ways. You have planted much, but have harvested little. You eat, but never have enough. You drink, but never have your fill. You put on clothes, but are not warm. You earn wages, only to put them in a purse with holes in it. ... You expected much, but see, it turned out to be little. What you brought home, I blew away. Why?" declares the Lord Almighty. "Because of my house, which remains a ruin, while each of you is busy with his own house" (NIV).

Do those outcomes sound familiar? Have you experienced this in your own life? Has all your busyness brought you real life satisfaction, or has it reduced the quality of your life? Have you reaped commensurate to what you've sown? Or is your experience closer to: "You have planted much, but have harvested little. ... You earn wages, only to put them in a purse with holes in it"?

If you're a busy person who's still finding yourself to be restless, dissatisfied, or frustrated with what your life has become, perhaps it's time to examine that temple of yours and reorder your life around God. Perhaps God has sent this study to be your Haggai, inviting you to finally put first things first.

Think About It

Haggai indicates that if we allow the busyness of life to distract us from God, we'll be prevented from enjoying a satisfying life. Might this be a root cause of why your life isn't all that you want it to be?

For Group Discussion

What sort of progress have you made throughout this study and what lessons from the Book of Haggai could help you to sustain that progress?

Talk to God About It

Read Haggai chapter 1 and notice something. After being admonished, the people quickly rebuilt the temple and God promised that He would be with them. No matter how long we've allowed ourselves to be distracted from God, He welcomes us back. Why not take a few minutes right now and commit to God that you'll rebuild your temple of relationship with Him, in full confidence that He'll rejoice?

Your Freedom from Busyness Plan, Part 20

Write down the most important thing you can do to ensure that the busyness of your life will never again undermine your relationship with God.

Introduction

Every Christian is called to be a leader.

Some are more gifted at leadership than others, but we worship a God who calls every one of us to influence the people around us—to lead them to a fuller understanding of Who God is, of what He's done for us, and how He wants us to live our lives.

The Great Commission is perhaps the clearest statement of our call to leadership (Matthew 28:18-20). It's reasonably straightforward, isn't it? Make disciples. Influence people. Love people enough to lead them from one place to another. Indeed, every Christian is called to be a leader.

Maybe you're approaching the leadership of this study with the utmost confidence. Maybe you've done this sort of thing before and you're pretty good at it. But if instead you're one of those people who's uneasy about leading a study because you think God has not specifically gifted you to lead others, try to set those concerns aside. That's not a biblical way of thinking about who God has made you to be. God does want you to be a discipler, an influencer—a leader—and He will give you the ability to facilitate well, if you ask Him.

What's Inside This Guide

This brief leader guide is intended to offer you some helpful hints about how to lead your small group or Sunday school class through this study, whether it's your first time or your hundred and first. After covering some general tips on the art of small group leadership, this guide will give you specific suggestions for how to lead each of the five sessions in this study. If read this guide closely and internalize its ideas, you'll find it to be a springboard to success in all of your meetings.

The Art of Leading a Small Group

There's been a lot written on how to lead a small group and how not to lead one. Here's a compilation of some of the best ideas out there—twenty tips that will assist you in leading your group to a life-changing experience.

Tip 1: It's Not About You. Let's get one thing straight from the beginning: leading a small group study is not about you. It's about God. The more you can remain in the mindset of magnifying God and minimizing yourself, the more others will learn from the study. Take a cue from John the Baptist: "He must increase, but I must decrease" (John 3:30).

For some small group leaders, this humble posture is quite natural. For others, the ego has a funny way of creeping into everything they do. If you find yourself saying and doing things out of concern for what others will think of you as the leader, that's a red flag. Instead, try not to worry about your reputation—about pleasing people, in Paul's words (Galatians 1:10). Your job as a small group leader is simply to co-labor with God to draw people closer to Him.

So, to boil it down to a sentence: to lead a small group with excellence, be the "guide on the side," not the "sage on the stage." This is God's group. Keep Him at center stage and He will bless everyone in the group.

Tip 2: Operate in God's Strength. Tip 1 said that great small-group leadership happens when you make the study *about God*. Here's the flip side: great small-group leadership also happens when you lead the study *through God*. The best leader is one who's first a follower of God. Ask God to empower you to lead beyond your abilities and return to this prayer often. Additionally, make prayer the bedrock of your group time together as well, at the very least opening and closing each session by collectively talking to God.

Tip 3: Operate in Joy. The leader's disposition powerfully drives the disposition of the whole group. If you adopt a joyful disposition throughout the study, others will follow. When you smile, when you're upbeat, when you're genuinely excited to be leading, when you celebrate successes, it will infect the group—and that will significantly improve the experience for everyone involved.

As you know, though, joy doesn't just happen. It's not something you can engineer on demand, nor can you fake for very long. Rather, real joy starts with seeing clearly the opportunity with which God has blessed you. You have been commissioned to help Him make the lives of people better through leading this study. Your work with this group is, in fact, *a sacred ministry*. This sort of perspective leads to gratitude for the opportunity and out of gratitude flows joy, both in your preparation and in your leadership of the discussion.

Tip 4: Encourage Accountability. Accountability matters, and because it matters, we see it in a lot of contexts. CEOs answer to boards. Accrediting bodies hold schools to high standards. Governments guard against excessive power of their branches by maintaining checks-and-balance systems.

Accountability matters in small groups as well. We're more likely to experience permanent change when we have an accountability partner who will support us, ask us whether we're keeping up with the studies, and check on our progress. So, early on, encourage people to walk through the study with at least one other person.

Tip 5: Preparation, Preparation and Preparation. In real estate the three most important things in a property are location, location and location. In small group leadership—and in teaching generally—one could piggyback on this axiom and say the three most important things are preparation, preparation and preparation. There's no substitute for it (as some of us have seen from witnessing an unprepared group leader or teacher.) If you're going to facilitate effectively, you need to have mapped out how you'll begin the group meeting, what questions you'll cover, approximately how much time you'll be devoting to each of them, some proposed answers for each question, and a way to bring the meeting to effective closure. In your planning, though, don't worry about becoming an expert on the subject matter. Great facilitation can easily happen even though you're not an expert on the topic (remember, you're a "guide on the side.") But it's unlikely to happen without planning and thorough preparation.

Tip 6: Model the Way. If you want people to listen to one another, then listen closely to people. If you want them to be transparent and candid, then you go first. If you want them to dig deeper to identify root causes of their problems, then model that yourself. If you want them to be account-able to one another, then be sure they know of your accountability relationship. Lead by example, not just by what you say.

Tip 7: Create a Safe Environment for Sharing. In almost any small-group, there will be people who are intimidated or shy about participating. There are some things you can do, though, to make it safe for them to engage. For starters, be transparent. Share your own struggles. Admit your own challenges with the issues being discussed. Confess your own imperfec-tions and others will feel freer to then share their own.

It's also important to be supportive early in the study of almost every comment. That doesn't mean you tolerate heresy, but it does mean signaling that people don't need to be profound to contribute something of value. Try to avoid strongly disagreeing with people until such a point when everyone feels comfortable contributing.

Along the same lines, it's also wise to remain sensitive to others' traditions. More and more, people are crossing denominational lines to participate in small-group studies. If you have an ecumenical small group, seek to understand where others are coming from and minimize the disparagement of other denominational perspectives. Of course, there will be times when it's appropriate to raise and examine these differences, but those discussions should probably be deferred until the group has matured a bit.

Tip 8: Hone Your Listening Skills. There's an old adage that says: "Being listened to is so close to being loved, that most people can't tell the difference." You may have experienced that feeling first-hand. Do what you can to make sure everyone in your group feels it as well.

Concentrate on what each person is saying, rather than thinking about your own response. Rephrase their point when appropriate, so they'll know they've been heard. Use non-verbal cues as well that show you're listening—cues like maintaining a comfortable level of eye contact with the person speaking, occasionally nodding, positioning your body to squarely face the speaker, leaning toward the speaker slightly, and so on. You'll be amazed at how such little things can make a person feel "listened to"—and loved!

Tip 9: Stay on Point. This is the bane of many small groups. One off-topic comment gives license to the next, and before you know it, a series of loosely related remarks has taken up your entire meeting time.

Ever been there? My guess is that you know exactly what I'm talking about, since this happens all too often.

This is a leadership problem. To avoid it, keep the group focused on the question at hand and follow up tangential comments by bringing the group back to the actual question. Everyone benefits when a leader steers the conversation, and everyone suffers when he or she does not.

Tip 10: Be Sure That Scripture Is Your Filter. One would think we wouldn't have to say such a thing, but it seems that sometimes our filters for right and wrong get clouded, even in Christian circles. Some people use their experience to judge right from wrong. Others use society's rules. Some are pragmatists, basing the right thing to do on what works.

There are a lot of worldviews infecting Christian thinking these days, so when group members suggest solutions to problems, don't shy away from asking whether their suggestion aligns with scripture. Ask them if Jesus did it that way, or would do it that way. Ask them for any biblical support they can think of.

If, as group leaders we persistently come back to the Bible as God's standard, our group members will too.

Tip 11: Listen for Segues to the Next Question. It's invaluable to always know where you want to go next with a discussion. Sometimes you simply have to announce the transition (e.g., "Let's turn a corner now and look at the next question."), but the meeting flows more smoothly if you capitalize on natural transition points. Expert facilitators listen closely for comments that connect to where they want to go next and quickly use those comments to move the discussion forward.

Tip 12: Echo What's Been Said. This is such an essential facilitation technique! From time to time, you'll find it helpful to restate what somebody has just said—to "echo" it for the group. Echoing not only lets the speaker know that he or she has been understood, it also serves to clarify that person's point for everyone else. Beyond that, echoing makes it more likely that the rest of the group will respond to that person's comment, rather than just following with an unrelated comment.

So echo comments where appropriate, and then, since you have the floor at that moment, invite commentary on what's just been said. The flow of discussion will improve dramatically.

Tip 13: Connect the Dots. Another way to enhance the flow of discussion is to connect some people's comments to other people's comments. "So Sherry, you think that the verse calls us to action but Fran, two minutes ago, you said you didn't understand it that way. Can somebody else help us out here?" This is good facilitation because it clarifies where we are with the discussion and where we want it to go.

Tip 14: Cut Off Dominators. Let's face it, they're out there. Many groups are blessed with that spirited person who contributes a little too much. And that can diminish the experience for everyone else. Usually, if the leader doesn't take control of this situation, no one will.

One solution is to talk to the person away from the group. It doesn't take much. Start by affirming the positive and then candidly make your request. "Hank, you really have a lot of good stuff to contribute in this study, but I want to make sure that others have an adequate opportunity to share, too. Would you be willing to scale back—at least a little—the number of times you contribute?"

A second way to balance contribution is to simply cut in when the domi-nator takes a breath, echo what he or she has said to that point (so they know they've been heard), and invite someone to respond to that. As a last resort, you might say to the group something like: "I don't want you to feel like you're in school, but in the interest of managing this discus-sion, it would help me if you all would raise your hand when you want to comment." Then regulate the dominator's contributions in a way that's more helpful to the group.

Tip 15: Ask for People's Opinions. "How 'bout somebody who hasn't spoken yet?" "Anyone else want to comment on this issue?" "Does anyone have a different perspective on this?" These and similar questions are non-threatening ways of inviting people into the conversation. Write out some phrases with which you're comfortable and use them at strategic points in your group meetings to draw in quiet group members. Sometimes just this little nudge can be a turning point for people.

Tip 16: Frame Questions Using "Why" and "How." Usually, when you ask a question that begins with "why" or "how," people tend to answer with more thoughtful, more extensive responses than if you ask a question that begins with "who," "where," or "when." Think about it. Questions that begin with these latter words can lend themselves to one or two word answers, right? But try answering a "why" or "how" question with one word. Not likely. If your goal is to get people talking, think about refram-ing the questions you ask.

Tip 17: Permit Silence After You Ask a Question. Eventually, it'll happen. You'll ask a question and no one will say anything. Avoid the temptation to fill that void with your own voice. Give people time to think. Let them muster the courage to answer a tough question. Give them a moment to hear from God, if that's the prompting they're seeking.

Get comfortable with silence after posing a question. Often, your patience will be rewarded with some of the richest and most poignant answers of the week.

Tip 18: Stay With Fruitful Conversation, Even If It's Taking Too Much Time.
For group leaders who are especially time-conscious, it's natural to march through a set of questions and make sure everything gets covered in the time allotted. The best group leaders remain mindful, though, that the *real* goal of the meetings *is transformation*, not efficiency or box-checking.

Sometimes a question will stimulate lots of discussion. It will go deep; it will touch a chord; it will create excitement; it will surface pains or misunderstandings that need to be addressed; it will plant the seeds of lasting change for people. Avoid cutting off God's work in these situations. Don't be a slave to a script, insisting on covering all five questions in ten minutes each. Some questions may require twenty minutes, others three minutes. So be flexible and learn to discern when to deviate from your original plan.

Tip 19: Use a Board or Easel, if Appropriate. Chronicling on a board the relevant points that people make is a wonderful way of affirming, echoing, and clarifying what's being said. It will also help you to "connect the dots" more easily. Beyond that, many people will retain more of what's said if they've both heard it and seen it in writing.

Tip 20: Summarize Key Points. Many people will find it instructive if you can recap some of the more important lessons from the discussion. The end of the session is a natural time to do this, but it's also helpful to do it at the beginning of a group meeting ("This is what God's taught us so far in this study."), as well as after particularly important or complicated points in the discussion. Brief, oral summaries from the leader enhance learning and retention, so take notes during the discussion and bless the group by emphasizing the essential take-aways.

Session 1

Suggested Structure for Session 1

- Open in prayer
- Group members introduce themselves (5-10 minutes)
- Leader distributes books and asks members to turn to the survey on pages 100-105 (5 minutes)
- Group members complete the "Obstacles to Growth Survey" on pages 100-105 and then discuss their insights from the assessment (15-25 minutes)
- Leader explains how this study works (5-10 minutes)
- Group watches a ten minute video to kick off the Week 1 studies (10 minutes)
- If there's time and interest, the group can cover the optional discussion question after the video (5-10 minutes)
- Close in prayer

Distribute the Books and Complete the Assessment Tool

As a special feature, this study includes a tool to help people diagnose the extent to which busyness is a problem. The tool, called the "Obstacles to Growth Survey," is intended to be completed by group members as the very first thing they do in Session 1. It's a 20 question survey that was scientifically designed at Regent University in Virginia, and it offers powerful insight into issues that inhibit one's relationship with God. Among those issues is the "busyness" of one's life, so participants will be able to see the extent to which busyness is an obstacle for them.

Members can find the "Obstacles to Growth Survey" in the back of their book, on pages 100-105. After distributing the books, have group members take about ten minutes to complete and score this survey. Then,

ask them how they did, especially with the obstacle of "busyness." If your group is typical of the thousands of Christians who have used this instrument, busyness will reveal itself as one of their largest obstacles to Christian growth. (Note: on this survey, the average busyness score for Christians is 5.4, whereas the averages for the other obstacles are 3.2 for "independence from God," 3.1 for "poor environment for growth," and 1.9 for "lack of knowledge about how to grow.")

Completing this assessment at the very beginning of this study is important because it helps people to see that they may indeed have a problem with the issue of busyness, and it may re-double their commitment to making this study a priority. It's also a fun, interactive ice-breaker for the group. They'll chuckle at the eye-opening results and, in all likelihood, see clearly the benefit of taking this study seriously.

Explain How This Study Works

Your explanation can be as long or short as you like. The approach of the study is reasonably self-explanatory, so as the leader, you won't need to go into tremendous detail at this point to get your group moving.

I'd suggest that you start by telling the group the overall purpose of the study—in a sentence, "to reduce the busyness and overload in your lives, so you have more time and energy for the things that matter most." As explained in the very first study of the book, "An Epidemic Among Christians":

> "It's not a study about managing your time better so you can get everything done. Neither is it intended to help you organize your activities so you can get more done in less time. There are plenty of very good "busyness management" resources on the market, if that's your goal. Instead, this study is about *busyness reduction*—permanent escape from the days of too much activity, too many responsibilities, too much hurry, and too little God."

The study is designed to be completed in four weeks with five small-group sessions. Session 1 is the beginning of Week 1 and then during the rest of Week 1, group members complete five daily studies on their own. In Session 2 (one week after Session 1), your group will discuss five questions—one from each of the five daily studies they just completed the previous week. In this way, group members have an opportunity to think through their answers to questions before the meeting where these questions are discussed.

Because folks going through this study tend to be "busy" people, I've designed the daily studies to be penetrating but brief. Each daily study should take about 10 to 15 minutes to complete. If time to read is a problem, suggest the use of the audio recording of the book to listen to or review the content. Emphasize to your group the importance of making time for their daily study, and suggest that they pair up with an account-ability partner in this study. Reinforcing this, Study 5 also encourages participants to seek out someone with whom they can walk through this study, and although the study can certainly be completed without pairing up, there is power in these sorts of "iron sharpening iron" relationships.

Weekly meetings should be about 60 to 75 minutes and, except for Session 1, they're intended to cover five discussion questions from the previous weeks' daily studies. After the discussion time, each meeting culminates with a ten minute video that lays a foundation for the coming week. If there's time and interest, you can also use the optional discussion question (presented in this Leader Guide) to invite the group to reflect on the video.

Another special feature of this study is a planning tool, called a "Freedom from Busyness" Plan. Each daily study not only invites participants to reflect on tough issues, it also poses an action-oriented question that's intended to help the participant create a plan to beat busyness. Collec-tively, these twenty questions over twenty studies comprise a plan—a set of goals and strategies for sustaining progress long after this study ends. Indicate to your group members how this planning tool works and the value of creating a plan, rather than just passively reading and discussing. On pages 106-109 there is a place to refine and collect all 20 parts of the "Freedom from Busyness" plan.

Watch the First Video

After you've shared your brief overview of the study, ask if anyone has any questions. Then show the first ten minute video that accompanies this study. The intention of each video is to set the stage for the five studies that your group members will complete during the upcoming week. The videos are brief but memorable and to the point, so your group should find them both entertaining and educational.

You may find that the group is intrigued enough by the video to want to react to it immediately after it ends, rather than just adjourn the meeting. If that's the case, I suggest using the "Optional Discussion Question" presented in this Leader Guide (alternatively, you could make up your own question or simply ask the group members whether they want to comment on the video.)

Sometimes you'll find that the most spirited part of the meeting happens as group members react to the video, so after it ends, don't be shy about asking whether people want to take a few minutes for discussion.

For Session 1 (and all group meetings), show the video toward the end of the meeting. In this first meeting, it might also make sense to introduce the presenter, Dr. Michael Zigarelli, by simply reading his bio from page 4 and showing them his photo on the back of the book.

Optional Discussion Question After the Video

The first video humorously compares Jesus' not-so-busy life with our overloaded, overscheduled lives, and it invites viewers to make the study a priority over the next month. After showing this video, consider posing this question to your group: "How would you like your life to be different six months from now because of this study?"

Session 2

Suggested Structure for Session 2

- Open in prayer
- Discuss the five questions from Week 1 studies (30-40 minutes)
- Group watches a ten minute video to kick off the Week 2 studies (10 minutes)
- If there's time and interest, the group can cover the optional discussion question after the video (5-10 minutes)
- Close in prayer

Leader Insights for Discussion Questions

From Study 1: What do you think God would like you to get out of this study? Write down one or two things here, and indicate whether you're really committed to partnering with God throughout this study to reach these goals.

Leader Insight: We start off with an easy-to-answer question to get people accustomed to dialoguing in the group. Expect some pretty vanilla responses at first—responses like: "Yes, God wants me to reduce the busyness of my life and focus on Him more. And yes, I'm committed to partnering with God to reach these goals." That sort of response is okay—and it's good for people to make a public commitment—but you may also find it helpful to ask group members to be specific. In other

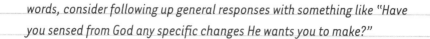

words, consider following up general responses with something like "Have you sensed from God any specific changes He wants you to make?"

From Study 2: How much has your prayer life improved in the past six months? How about in the past year? If it's not improving, is it because you've been too busy or distracted to talk with God?

Leader Insight: Unlike the previous question, this is a challenging question because for many people in your group the honest answer will be "no, my prayer life has not improved." This is a problem because so often, the quality of our prayer life is among the best indicators of the quality of our relationship with God. If the former is stagnant, in all likelihood, so is the latter.

Many people are distracted from God—so busy with the ordinary things of life that their relationship with God has become a low priority. As people admit that God is getting crowded out of their life, this public admission can be a turning point for them. Be supportive and em- pathetic. And be sure not to let group members even imply a hint of judgment on one another at this early stage of the study. You need to create a safe environment for people to share candidly.

From Study 3: Consider the statement "priorities are what we do." Think about what you do—where your time goes in a typical day. How much of a "priority" is it for you to delight your spouse and to make your marriage as good as God wants it to be?

Leader Insight: This is not a comfortable question for some, so tread carefully. Some people have a lot of marital baggage, so they don't want to even think about "delighting" their spouse and may object to the theology behind this question. Others have never thought in terms of "delighting" their spouse because no one's taught them they should. This can be a real learning opportunity, if facilitated well. To do that, ask someone to speak first who you know has a successful marriage and who believes that developing our marriages should be high priority for us. This will help affirm the legitimacy of "delighting" our spouses and keep the discussion focused on a Biblical view of marriage, rather than an objector's view of marriage.

From Study 4: How is the busyness of your life affecting your ability to serve others joyfully and well?

Leader Insight: Many people in the group no doubt will be people who serve a lot. Whether at home, in the workplace, in the church or elsewhere, chances are you'll have more than a few in the room with "compassion fatigue." They continue to serve, but may do it without much joy.

Let that become apparent in this brief discussion, perhaps by soliciting a story or two from the group about how a busy life is stealing the joy of serving others. No need to try to solve the problem now—that's what this study's about—but help people see clearly that busyness is an enemy of joy.

From Study 5: A lot of Christians throughout the centuries have indicated that we're more likely to experience permanent change when we have an accountability partner who can support us and ask us the tough questions. What do you think?

Leader Insight: "Accountability" is a word that we need to reclaim as Christians. Some people hear it negatively, inferring that it entails being controlled or monitored. But from a Biblical perspective, accountability is very positive since it's such a powerful pathway to growth.

To demonstrate this, it would be wise to raise to the surface any stories people have about breakthrough experiences they've had because of a mentor / accountability partner. This not only evidences the power of accountability, it should encourage people to take seriously the call to action in this study to partner-up with someone. If you think it's appropriate, ask people in the group whether they need an accountability partner for this study to pray with them, encourage them, and keep them on track.

Optional Discussion Question After the Video

The second video is about intentionally making space in our lives by saying no to more things. After showing this video, consider posing this question to your group: "What's your initial reaction to the idea of saying no more often to requests for your time?"

Session 3

Suggested Structure for Session 3

- Open in prayer
- Discuss the five questions from Week 2 studies (30-40 minutes)
- Group watches a ten minute video to kick off the Week 3 studies (10 minutes)
- If there's time and interest, the group can cover the optional discussion question after the video (5-10 minutes)
- Close in prayer

Leader Insights for Discussion Questions

From Study 6: What are your biggest obstacles to saying no to requests for your time, and what might you do to overcome those obstacles?

Leader Insight: Have participants dig deep to identify the real obstacles. They may claim reasons beyond their control like: "my kids need me" or "my company insists that I say yes to everything." But beneath those answers may be deeper reasons that are not beyond their control. The deeper reasons might be things like "I don't know how to say no to my kids" or "I'm seeking to be move up the corporate ladder, so I need to impress all the top decision-makers at work." Be willing to probe a bit to help diagnose the real issues, and then explore some potential solutions. There's no sense in just treating the symptoms.

From Study 7: Saying no to serving others is appropriate if God first gives us permission to say no to them. How will you know whether God is giving you permission to say no to a request for your time?

Leader Insight: This is really a question about hearing God, one of the most challenging issues of all for people. There probably will be people in the group who are not confident that they've ever heard from God on anything, so deferring to some of the more spiritually mature people in the room to explain how they hear God could create a life-changing moment for some group members.

From Study 8: Whether you'd label yourself a perfectionist or not, consider the central question in today's study: is "people-pleasing" part of what's driving your busy, overloaded schedule? If so, write down and share a few specific examples of when this has happened.

Leader Insight: Our desire to look good in others' eyes is a primary driver of our overload. If we could just set aside these reputation concerns, many people would immediately eliminate all of their busyness problems. So take time with this question in your group.
It might also be a good time to try to draw in quieter members of the group since it's such a pervasive problem that almost everyone will have some sort of answer.

From Study 9: Consider the parenting guidance "say yes when you can and no when you must." It's easy to go too far in one direction or the other, especially when making adjustments to your parenting style. How can you maintain a proper balance, so that you're not saying yes too often or no too often?

Leader Insight: There's no cookie-cutter answer here. There may be some people in your group with a lot of parenting experience, and if so, it would be wise to tap their expertise on this issue.

Also, you might want to suggest to the group that talking regularly about balanced parenting with one's spouse is an invaluable part of effective child rearing. God put men and women together to be a parenting team, so we should defer to His design and ask our spouse regularly whether we're being too lenient or too strict.

From Study 10: Jot down the television programs you watch regularly. If Jesus sat down on the couch next to you while you were watching any of these, would you change the channel?

Leader Insight: Don't miss this question because of time constraints. It's well worth the discussion because of its unusually powerful im-agery. Ask if anyone's willing to admit that they watch programs that they might not want Jesus to watch with them.

Also, explore the central issue of this daily study—whether too much TV is a time thief that's making the rest of their life too busy. With Americans averaging three hours of TV watching a day, there's bound to be someone in your group for whom this question is the most important question of the study.

Optional Discussion Question After the Video

The third video is about having so much to do in life that we rush through our relationships with God and others, mentally putting them on a to-do list. After showing this video, consider posing this question to your group: "How big of a problem is 'checklist Christianity' for you?"

Session 4

Suggested Structure for Session 4

- Open in prayer
- Discuss the five questions from Week 3 studies (30-40 minutes)
- Group watches a ten minute video to kick off the Week 4 studies (10 minutes)
- If there's time and interest, the group can cover the optional discussion question after the video (5-10 minutes)
- Close in prayer

Leader Insights for Discussion Questions

From Study 11: In what situations is hurry adversely affecting your relationships and/or your witness? Or think about it this way: if Jesus were you for one day, with what activities would He take more time?

Leader Insight: The latter question is more powerful, so you may want to focus attention there. Regardless where you start, though, expect people to feel both a little overwhelmed and a little remorseful when answering. Be empathetic. Hurry is a relationship killer and as people come to grips with how it's stolen away quality time with loved ones, they'll likely be frustrated and disappointed. If that's the case, encourage them to use

that frustration to finally eliminate hurry from their lives.
Also encourage group members to commit to their accountability
partner that they'll take more time with at least one specific activity
this week. Allow people the opportunity to share with the group what
that one activity will be, if they desire.

From Study 12: What does your typical Sabbath look like and how rested
do you feel at the beginning of the next day? What are some activities of
your typical Sabbath that might be better left for another day?

*Leader Insight: You should receive a lot of response to this question
because chances are, everyone's thought about the issue long before
coming into this study. Christians know that the Sabbath's a special day
and that we should set it aside as such, but still we seldom live differently on the Sabbath. Group members' responses to the question of how
rested they feel the beginning of the next day will attest to that.*

*Take time to really deal with the question of acceptable and unaccept-
able Sabbath activities, but not in a legalistic way. Show the group
that ultimately, embracing the wisdom that rest is a holy activity will
lead to experiencing the kind of Sabbath that God intends.*

From Study 13: Respond to the closing questions of this study: What
would it take for you to discipline your thought life so you could live in the
moment and give people your complete, undivided attention? How much
less stressful would your life be if you focused on one thing at a time?
How much better would your relationships be if you did? And how much
more would people see Jesus in you?

*Leader Insight: Those who don't live in the moment will squander the
life God's given them. They'll enjoy life a lot less, their relationships
will be under-developed and they will often be anxious. Get real practical with this question so people have a clear take-away. Ask people*

who have succeeded in this area how they've disciplined their minds to turn off concern about the past or the future, to be fully present to the people around them. Glean especially from the members of the group who may have learned this lesson the hard way.

From Study 14: As indicated in today's study, "prayer" is different from "saying prayers." We can think of "prayer" as mindfulness of God or being "God-conscious." How God-conscious are you in a typical day, and what could you do to become more God-conscious in everything you do—to move toward the New Testament ideal of praying always?

Leader Insight: This is breakthrough theology for many people, so don't gloss over it. It will lift a tremendous weight off of people who have for years been feeling guilty about their prayer life. So spend time listening to any revelations people have had because of this day's study.

Identify practical things people do to remain God-conscious. Habitually listening to Christian radio, keeping verses or Christian pictures in front of them at work and home, and using Christian screen savers on the computer, are but a few of the many possible ideas.

From Study 15: E-mail, instant messaging, and other electronic media can be wonderful tools, when used with discretion. But as indicated in this study, they can also adversely affect our relationships. How, if at all, have your relationships been adversely affected by electronic communications?

Leader Insight: This question lends itself very nicely to stories, and almost everyone who uses e-mail can tell such a story. So seek one or two as you close out this discussion and then link this discussion to the previous one by asking whether e-mailing people can be prayer. You see, the medium is not really the problem. How we use the medium is the problem.

Before the video, assign the group to individually refine and collect the steps of the *Freedom from Busyness* Plan from each day's study, writing them on to pages 106-109 before the Session 5 meeting.

Optional Discussion Question After the Video

The fourth video is about how our culture can shape us to think and act in secular ways, including overworking and overspending. We're too busy, in part, because we're living like so many people around us.

After showing this video, consider posing this question to your group: "Why do people believe that the more we get the happier we'll be, and how does that belief keep us living the over-extended life?"

Session 5

Suggested Structure for Session 5

- Open in prayer
- Discuss the five questions from Week 4 studies (30-40 minutes)
- Group watches a ten minute video to complete the study (10 minutes)
- Take time for group reflection on the "Freedom from Busyness" experience
- Close in prayer

NOTE: This is the fifth and final group meeting. Consider making it a celebration of sorts, with snacks and refreshments. The suggested structure is identical to previous weeks, but you may also want to consider using some time after the video for people to reflect on the experience and to publicly commit to pursuing lasting change in their life.

Leader Insights for Discussion Questions

From Study 16: Look over that simplicity list in this study. How many of these items describe you? And what does your answer tell you about the potential for improvement in your life?

Leader Insight: This is a good ice-breaker question for this final week. Many people will readily admit that very few items in the simplicity list describe them at all. That's both humorous and tragic. And it implicates the enormous opportunity for improvement.

Remind the group of one of the study's major points: simplicity begins on the inside, by having a divine center. Encourage your group not to begin with outward simplicity (i.e., the things on the simplicity list), but with the inward simplicity of true God-centeredness that leads to gratitude and contentment (as indicated in the study that follows this one.)

From Study 17: When you think about the quality of your life, what's your benchmark? In other words, against what or whom do you measure your quality of life? We often do this by comparing ourselves to someone who lives near us, or to what our life was like in the past. As a result, no matter what we have, we tend not to see our life as terribly abundant. But what if our benchmark were a single parent in a Brazilian slum or a refugee in the Sudan or a homeless person in the next city? How would that frame of reference change your thinking and your ability to live a simpler life?

Leader Insight: This will be an epiphany for some people in your group. Our frame of reference has remarkable power to affect our content-ment—and ultimately how much we busy ourselves pursuing things. Don't let people off the hook here. If they've made it this far in the

study, they can handle being pressed a bit for how they determine whether they have enough in life. Pay particular attention to people in the group who have gone on a missions trip to some destitute area and have come back changed. They can teach the group much about how to have a theology of enough and how that leads to a simpler, less overloaded life.

From Study 18: How often do you think about the issue of stewardship when you're spending money? What could you do to maintain a stewardship mindset all the time?

Leader Insight: Some people may put a picture of Jesus in their wallet or their checkbook—a picture that they can see every time they open it. Some may keep stewardship verses before them, until a stewardship mentality has become a habit. Brainstorm creative ideas with your group because if people can make this change in mindset, a lot of other things in their life, including their busyness and overload, will change.

From Study 19: Being a workaholic, whether you're paid for your work or not, is one of the scourges of contemporary Christian life. Many Christians work too much. Do you? How do you know if you have a problem?

Leader Insight: Remember, it's not just ambitious people climbing the corporate ladder or folks working for slave-driving bosses who are "workaholics." A lot of stay-at-home moms fit this category as well. They've adopted a lifestyle of constant motion, satisfying one responsibility after another. They are fabulous servants, but unhealthy Christians because they work too much.

People may be quick to tell you that others in their life work too much, but rationalize the amount that they themselves work, so drill down to see whether they've in fact asked anyone whether they too have succumbed to the "obstacle of overwork."

From Study 20: What sort of progress have you made throughout this study and what lessons from the Book of Haggai could help you to sustain that progress?

> *Leader Insight: Haggai is a powerful little book because it could have been written yesterday. In any generation, ignoring God has an enormous number of adverse consequences. One of those consequences in our day is an overloaded life spent chasing the things that the world considers important.*
>
> *That lesson in itself could eclipse almost everything else in this book. Busyness is not just about wrong priorities on the outside. Often, it traces its roots to wrong priorities on the inside. Ultimately, we won't make lasting progress with our busyness problem until we make lasting progress in our relationship with God.*

Discussion After the Video

Encourage the group to utilize their Freedom from Busyness plan. Collecting all 20 parts of their plan from the end of each daily study and compiling them on pages 106-109 will make this easier to do.

Point out that the fifth video also offers several practical tips to help keep the "weight" of busyness off our lives for good. At the end of the video is a call to action—an invitation to make a public commitment to never return to the overloaded life. Inviting people to respond to that call may be an ideal way to close the study in your group. As people respond with their commitment, consider having the group pray for them and then, after everyone's been prayed for, celebrate together!

THE OBSTACLES TO GROWTH SURVEY

The *Obstacles to Growth Survey* is a tool to help you understand some of the obstacles that may stand in the way of your spiritual growth. By "spiritual growth" we simply mean growing toward godliness in your daily life—in all that you think, say, and do. As a Christian-based instrument, the assumptions underlying this tool are rooted in Christian scripture and theology. However, the survey is designed for use by both Christians and non-Christians.

For best results, please follow these instructions when completing the OGS:

INSTRUCTIONS

The *Obstacles to Growth Survey* will be most useful to you if you do not rush through the form, if you think about the questions carefully before answering, and if you provide accurate answers, to the best of your ability. It should take you about 5-10 minutes to complete.

After you have answered all 20 questions, use the scoring key at the end of the form to compute your scores.

Part 1: Indicate the extent to which you agree with the following statements

	Strongly Disagree	Disagree		Neither Agree nor Disagree		Agree		Strongly Agree		A	B	C	D
	1	2	3	4	5	6	7	8	9				
1. There are people close to me who love God with all of their heart	1	2	3	4	5	6	7	8	9			(shaded)	
2. To grow spiritually requires that a person make growth a top priority in life	1	2	3	4	5	6	7	8	9		(shaded)		
3. I would say that I am a God-centered person	1	2	3	4	5	6	7	8	9	(shaded)			
4. The person closest to me would assist me if I wanted to improve my spiritual growth	1	2	3	4	5	6	7	8	9				
5. The person closest to me loves God with all of his or her heart	1	2	3	4	5	6	7	8	9			(shaded)	
6. Spiritual growth should be more important to people than it is	1	2	3	4	5	6	7	8	9			(shaded)	
7. It is a high priority for me to try to please God in all that I do	1	2	3	4	5	6	7	8	9	(shaded)			
8. The pain in a person's life is an opportunity to grow spiritually	1	2	3	4	5	6	7	8	9				
9. Praying often is necessary for spiritual growth	1	2	3	4	5	6	7	8	9		(shaded)		
10. The people closest to me are more spiritually mature than I am	1	2	3	4	5	6	7	8	9			(shaded)	

Part 2: Indicate the extent to which each statement is true of you

	Never true of me	Rarely true of me	Sometimes true of me	Often true of me	Always true of me	A	B	C	D
11. The people closest to me encourage me to grow spiritually	1	2 3	4	5 6 7	8 9			▨	
12. To grow spiritually, one should regularly practice the "spiritual disciplines"	1	2 3	4	5 6 7	8 9		▨		
13. I rush from task to task	1	2 3	4	5 6 7	8 9				▨
14. I eat quickly	1	2 3	4	5 6 7	8 9				▨
15. I turn to God when making choices (reverse-scored question)	9	8 7	6	5 4 3	2 1	▨			
16. I feel guilty when I relax	1	2 3	4	5 6 7	8 9				▨
17. I act as if what God thinks of me is more important than what people think of me (reverse-scored question)	9	8 7	6	5 4 3	2 1	▨			
18. When I do not need to hurry, I tend to hurry anyway	1	2 3	4	5 6 7	8 9				▨
19. I am exhausted at the end of my day	1	2 3	4	5 6 7	8 9				▨
20. I do God's will (reverse-scored question)	9	8 7	6	5 4 3	2 1	▨			

Scoring Your Form

Step 1: Add the shaded boxes for each column

Step 2: Divide each sum by 5 to compute your scores (simply use the Division Table below)

Step 3: Interpret your score using the interpretation table below

	Sum for Column	Sum divided by 5	Obstacle to Growth
COLUMN A			This indicates how much *Independence from God* is an obstacle to your growth
COLUMN B			This indicates how much *lack of knowledge about how to grow* is an obstacle to your growth
COLUMN C			This indicates how much *an unsupportive environment for growth* is an obstacle to your growth
COLUMN D			This indicates how much *busyness* is an obstacle to your growth

DIVISION TABLE

Divided by 5		Divided by 5		Divided by 5		Divided by 5	
5	1.0	16	3.2	27	5.4	38	7.6
6	1.2	17	3.4	28	5.6	39	7.8
7	1.4	18	3.6	29	5.8	40	8.0
8	1.6	19	3.8	30	6.0	41	8.2
9	1.8	20	4.0	31	6.2	42	8.4
10	2.0	21	4.2	32	6.4	43	8.6
11	2.2	22	4.4	33	6.6	44	8.8
12	2.4	23	4.6	34	6.8	45	9.0
13	2.6	24	4.8	35	7.0		
14	2.8	25	5.0	36	7.2		
15	3.0	26	5.2	37	7.4		

Freedom from Busyness

Interpreting Your Obstacles to Growth Scores

The *Obstacles to Growth Survey* measures some of the larger obstacles to spiritual growth that many people experience (there are, of course, many other obstacles). Please note that your scores represent an estimate of the potential for each obstacle to limit your spiritual growth. The higher the number, the greater the obstacle may be for you.

Please use this table to interpret your scores:

Below 2.0	This is probably not an obstacle for you.
2.0 to 3.9	This may be a moderate obstacle for you. You should examine further, perhaps with the assistance of people who know you well, to assess whether this issue is in fact limiting your spiritual growth.
4.0 to 5.9	This may be a significant obstacle for you. If so, it is an obstacle that requires your attention. Consider addressing this obstacle soon if you want to grow.
6.0 or greater	This may be a severe obstacle for you. If so, it is likely an obstacle that is preventing you from making much progress in the area of spiritual growth.

MY FREEDOM FROM BUSYNESS PLAN

Part 1.

Part 2.

Part 3.

Part 4.

Part 5.

Part 6.

Part 7.

Part 8.

Part 9.

Part 10.

Part 11.

Part 12.

Part 13.

Part 14.

Part 15.

Part 16.

Part 17.

Part 18.

Part. 19

Part 20.

Audio Book Menu and Guide

If you are truly busy, a drive-time reviewer, or sight-impaired, here are the 20 daily studies and the daily questions, read by author Mike Zigarelli and Pam Case, respectively, in audio CD format for your convenience.

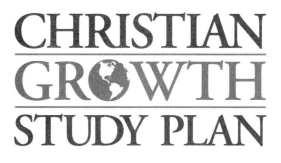

CHRISTIAN GROWTH STUDY PLAN

In the **Christian Growth Study Plan (formerly Church Study Course)**, this book *Freedom from Busyness* is a resource for course credit in the subject area Personal Life of the Christian Growth category of plans. To receive credit, read the book, complete the learning activities, show your work to your pastor, a staff member or church leader, then complete the following information. This page may be duplicated. Send the completed page to:

Christian Growth Study Plan · One LifeWay Plaza · Nashville, TN 37234-0117
FAX: (615)251-5067 · E-mail: *cgspnet@lifeway.com*

For information about the Christian Growth Study Plan, refer to the Christian Growth Study Plan Catalog. It is located online at *www.lifeway.com/cgsp*. If you do not have access to the Internet, contact the Christian Growth Study Plan office (1.800.968.5519) for the specific plan you need for your ministry.

FREEDOM FROM BUSYNESS: BIBLICAL HELP FOR OVERLOADED PEOPLE
CG-1169

PARTICIPANT INFORMATION

Social Security Number (USA ONLY-optional)	Personal CGSP Number*	Date of Birth (MONTH, DAY, YEAR)
– –	–	– –

Name (First, Middle, Last)	Home Phone
	–

Address (Street, Route, or P.O. Box)	City, State, or Province	Zip/Postal Code

Email Address for CGSP use

Please check appropriate box: ❑ Resource purchased by church ❑ Resource purchased by self ❑ Other

CHURCH INFORMATION

Church Name

Address (Street, Route, or P.O. Box)	City, State, or Province	Zip/Postal Code

CHANGE REQUEST ONLY

☐ Former Name

☐ Former Address	City, State, or Province	Zip/Postal Code

☐ Former Church	City, State, or Province	Zip/Postal Code

Signature of Pastor, Conference Leader, or Other Church Leader	Date

*New participants are requested but not required to give SS# and date of birth. Existing participants, please give CGSP# when using SS# for the first time. Thereafter, only one ID# is required. **Mail to:** Christian Growth Study Plan, One LifeWay Plaza, Nashville, TN 37234-0117. Fax: (615)251-5067.

Revised 4-05